# OMG CANCER

## CAROLINE FERNANDEZ

Cancer at 17, married at 22, widowed at 23 and re-married at 27... Crazy.... To all readers, please read about my life with passion, excitement and a smile on your face, as this is how I lived it.

# FORWARD

When Caz phoned me to say that she'd written a book I didn't bat an eyelid. To be honest it wouldn't faze me if she called to say she was running for Prime Minister, but I must admit I was totally surprised when she said that she wanted me to write the foreword to her book. I panicked and told her that I didn't think I was up to the job, I'd never written a foreword before. Her attitude was "I've never written a book before." I guess you can't argue with that, also you don't win many arguments with Caz.

I first met Caz back in 2002 at a Teenage Cancer Trust gig at the Royal Albert Hall, and even though she was in remission, she certainly wasn't the stereotypical image that most people would associate with the term "teenage cancer patient". She was so confident and full of life and in many ways she typified the Teenage Cancer Trust ethos which is "teenager first, cancer patient second".

I don't want to give too much away, but having read her book I realised that I only knew half of Caz's story and it's typical of her that I laughed more times than I cried. There is a big part of me that wished she'd never had to endure so much at such a young age, but those experiences have played a part in making her the person she is and the person we all love.

Neil Smith RIP

Caz I'm so glad that you have found happiness – you deserve it.

Des Murphy

Co-Producer of Concerts for the Teenage Cancer Trust at the Royal Albert Hall & member of the Penguin Café Orchestra.

# 1 OMG CANCER

When you hear the word cancer, what's the first thing you think about?? As an adult, you think instant death with no reprieve. As a teenager, your mind goes wild with thoughts of sickness, balding, skinniness, drugs and then instant death.

However, in today's society the label 'Cancer' does not have to be all doom and gloom. Medicines have advanced to an extreme level, scientists are constantly developing new drugs and new techniques to save our lives.

My story is far from doom and gloom, my experience of Cancer was and still is a rollercoaster. It involves a lot of smiles, laughing, tears, (some of which were from laughing so hard) and in the next breath pain, suffering, torture and sadness. I have experienced far too much in my lifetime, but I've loved every minute and I wouldn't change a thing.

## 2 THIS IS ME..

When I woke up this morning and decided that today is the day I would write my book, I was not really sure where to start or how long it will take. However, they say when you start you just can't stop...

Many people ask me about my experiences and I am happy to talk about them...I mean I talk loads and when I get chatting there is no stopping me, so this feels like a great time to inspire the world with my story....

I think it is important to tell you a little bit about myself and what I was like before my whirlwind picked me up, span me round and spat me out. As hard as it is for many of my friends and family to believe, I used to be a very shy person. My social and communication skills were not much to be desired and the only time I was able to be my true self was when I was performing on stage in my roller-skates. When my skates came off, I found it difficult to communicate with people of my own age.

Growing up, I had a relatively normal life: I was a brownie, had swimming lessons and I was a good student at school. I think it's safe to say I have had a fab upbringing, my family were great, me and my brother argued like cats and dogs but we still got on. I feel the only real problem I had growing up was my fashion sense!!

My personality has always been very strong and independent. Growing up with a big brother helped me to toughen up and stand up for myself. I remember being bullied at school in my English lessons, or I should say, I remember a few boys trying to bully me. These boys would constantly take the mickey out of me and kick the back of my chair, though I knew how to handle myself.

At our school, we had a thing called muffty day; it was a day we got to wear our own clothes and express who we really were. However, as usual they started at the beginning of the lesson. So, in the middle of the class, I stood up, grabbed my folder, whisked myself round the desk and proceed to smack all three of the boys around their heads.... Oh, the feeling of strength, relief and power was amazing. From that day, I never had any bother during my school period, I think they were afraid of me!!!

My school life was not a lot to be desired, I didn't make many friends and as far as my teachers were concerned I wasn't very intelligent; apparently I was not a "high achiever"....... If only they could see me now! There were a few subjects I really enjoyed, but unfortunately, my teachers were not very encouraging. For example, my food tech teacher didn't like my brother as he was a really good cook, (he's a chef now) so she instantly took a disliking to me because of him (her loss as my cakes are amazing)! Sadly my textiles teacher thought my mum did all my work for me as she is a seamstress, and predicted me a C for my GCSE exam, so I went and got an A just for good measure. Luckily, she wasn't marking my work. My practical lessons seemed to be the only subjects where my skills really shone through. The only teacher who encouraged me academically was my English teacher and it wasn't until I left school that I understood why. Within the last five years I have been diagnosed with dyslexia. Reading, writing and my battle with excess comma usage is still a day to day struggle,,,,,,,,,,,,, but Mr. O'Rielly had faith in me. He decided not to tell me I was dyslexic until I left school, as he knew I would never be able to achieve the grades I needed for college. However, when I reached college I got tested and got all the help I needed to understand how my brain works and how I need to learn. Mr. O'Rielly was the best teacher at my secondary school and I owe my teaching degree to him.

Out of school, I loved my music, playing both the keyboard and clarinet to death at home. I was a member of a woodwind band at school, which I enjoyed, and I got to play my keyboard every single day (with the head phones on as to not annoy everyone). I also loved roller-skating. As a youngster I was in pantomimes, dressing up as many mystical creatures from a sunflower, villager to a mouse soldier and a futuristic punk rocker, which I might add, I think I was the most happy go lucky punk rocker ever... lol

When I was about 11, my dad changed his job, which meant we had to move towns from Hastings to Kent. This meant I had to change skating clubs and I started doing competitions. Mind you, I've never really been the competitive type, so I never really went out to win a competition, just to skate my bottom off and have loads of fun. Truthfully, if I could still skate today I would.

I have always had a very close and loving immediate family, we have always got on and I am sure that my life experiences would be completely different if we didn't. This year my folks have been happily married for 40 years, and my brother and his wife Clare are creeping up to 9 years.

I know one day I'll get there with my lovely hubby. It may sound boring and mundane to have a happy normal upbringing, but it was great and we didn't really have any drama in our family. We were normal, but no one could have predicted what was to happen.

# 3 DIAGNOSIS

This is me at 16 ready to rule the world.

At 16 I decided to go to college, which was a big turning point for me, as I felt as though I was able to become my own person. I enrolled to study hair and beauty therapy. I was certain my parents were slightly unsure about my decision; however, I really fancied something different. My first year of college was interesting; I learnt so much myself and made some really good friends. Of course we had the usual college experiences of going out, drinking far too much, having parties whilst trying to complete our course work and we absolutely loved dancing so at every given chance we got, we danced our feet off. I felt that college was my opportunity to develop into an adult and learn about responsibility, get qualified and truly start my life. I did not expect what was to come next.

It wasn't until the end of the school year in March when I started feeling pains in my left leg. These pains were an ache, which never went away, but I just thought I should lay off the roller-skating for a while. Waking up one morning around April/ May time the ache turned into a small lump in my left thigh muscle. Now, I have roller-skated my whole life, so I just presumed the little lump was a knot in my muscle, thus I and my mother rubbed deep heat on the affected area to ease the discomfort for weeks. Unfortunately, the lump continued to grow.

At the age of 16 a week felt like year, so over the few weeks the lump grew it felt like an eternity. When I got used to the aching, I kinda forgot about it a little and it wasn't until I was rubbing my hands down my legs one day that I felt that the solid mass had grown on my thigh. It was the size of my hand and had wrapped itself around the inside of my leg. At this stage, I thought I'd better mention it to my folks so we could

9

go to the doctors. My mum and I decided that it was time to ring the doctors, as the aching mass in my leg did not seem right. It took a few days to get an appointment, though when I got there my doctor took one look at it and said, "There is definitely something there that shouldn't be there, and I want to refer you for X-ray!" So, two weeks later I went for an X-ray with my mum. During these two weeks I just went back to normal life, I didn't really think about the upcoming X-ray, it's almost like I had no attachment to it, like it wasn't me.

I don't know if you have been to a hospital to have an X-ray, but once you've had your X-ray a doctor will then take a look at it and then call you in to let you know the outcome. Sitting in the waiting room, I watched several doctors going into the room where my X-ray was, very swiftly followed by the same doctors leaving the room with very concerned looks on their faces. This didn't worry me, though I'm pretty sure my mum was shitting herself.

After about 30 minutes of waiting, we were called in to see the doctor. He had my X-ray up on the light-box and I could tell by the look on his face that he knew what was wrong with me. The atmosphere was silent and cold, it was like that moment when you walk into a room and say, "who's died!" Little did I know, he was looking at me like the walking dead! Now at this point I felt fine within myself, as far as I was concerned I was fit, healthy and reasonably normal. However, he proceeded to tell my mum and I that he did not feel qualified to give us a diagnosis, though he believed that I had a bone tumor. Great....It's not very often you come a across a doctor who admits defeat before we've crossed the start line. I knew that we were going to be at the hospital for some time. My mum looked inquisitive, she looked as though someone had asked her a really hard question and she was trying to think of the answer, like putting the puzzle pieces together. He then said, "I have made a call to the orthopedic department downstairs and they are waiting to see you." So, me and my mum made our way downstairs to see another doctor.

My leg was quite sore and the walk seemed to take forever. The corridor appeared to get longer with every step we took. It was a quiet walk; I could tell my mum was nervous but she never really expressed how she felt. I wasn't really scared; I just wanted it all over and done with. When we finally arrived, it was different.

There was a Nurse waiting at the entrance to the orthopedic department, ready to take me straight through to see the doctor. She greeted us with the biggest smile and the bubbliest hello, which made us feel at ease, and then escorted to our designated room. I think this Doctors name was Dr Housden but I'm not 100% sure. Now, he was a lovely man; his bedside manner was brill (if I compare it to all the doctors that met over the years), he dealt with my teenage attitude, oh and he was wearing a funky tie.

This Dr Housden chap did a few tests on me, which consisted of bending my knee, straightening my leg and crouching whilst stood on the floor, and his conclusion was the same as the last doctor: he felt I had a bone tumor. After all of this I was completely calm, probably because I still had no idea what was going on. I was oblivious; at 16 the only cares you have are hair, makeup and whether or not your outfit was ok.... I don't think I was in denial, perhaps a little naïve, but who wasn't at 16.

Whilst we sat in the room, the doctor made a phone call to one of his colleagues in London, Proff Tim Briggs, who I like to call "Briggsy". What we didn't realise was that he was on the phone to an orthopaedic specialist who he studied with many years ago and just so happened to still be in touch with him. The only part of conversation that we overheard was the doctor saying, "Briggs, I have a very lovely young lady who needs your help, when can you fit her in." He came back to us with an appointment date and time on a piece of paper to go and see this doctor in London; it was like two days' time.......

I don't really remember having any thoughts or feelings at this point. I was a 16 year old stroppy teenager with an over protective family that didn't really listen to anything anyone said or did what anyone told me.... all I really knew was that I had a bone tumor. "Der.... What was a bone tumor???" The flies on the wall were shouting at me... I didn't see any severity in anything but that was just me... away with the fairies! As for my family, they didn't really use words...... just facial expressions, which were an easy to read book... sad, scared, nervous and fearful.

Numerous tests and scans were ordered; the biopsy was my first experience of true excruciating pain I had ever felt. My dad took me to the Royal National Orthopaedic Hospital in London for day surgery. They had to knock me out to do the biopsy, as they had to go deep into the bone. All they had to do was stick a massive needle straight into the centre of the tumor and suck a bit out, to determine exactly what was inside my leg.

When I came round they had stuck a plaster over my little wound, and at the time I didn't realise that I would be allergic to the plaster, but it would seem that within an hour I had two massive blisters either side of my little hole. I think I was more pissed off at the blister than the fact I had this thing growing in my leg. I suppose it was because I could actually see it and touch it and the thing in my leg was not visible.

During the days following the biopsy, the pain was interesting; I had an awful throbbing sensation running though my leg with a spiky tingling feeling which sprinkled over my left foot... it was relentless..... For the first time I was experiencing pain. For a while, I couldn't walk properly. At the time I compared it being shot in the leg; hopefully I never actually experience that though.

A couple of weeks passed and it was time to take a trip to London to get my results from the all the poking, prodding and bone picture taking I had been through. However, not only was it diagnosis day, but it was my birthday and I was turning 17.

Apparently the only birthday present I was getting was my doctor telling me I had a bone tumor in my left leg. Oh, and just to top off the overwhelming desire to scream, he explained my tumor had spread to my lungs.....tut tut... What an inconvenience!... It took me 30 seconds to process this information, after which I looked at my mum who was in tears, then glanced at my dad who had his saddest look on his face. I felt so much sadness in the room. I felt numb; I had never seen my family like this. The last time I saw my mum cry was probably when she popped me out, and as for my dad, he's the guy with all the jokes and friendly personality.

I have always looked to my dad for the answers; whatever the question he knew everything, though it seemed this time he was lost for words. Who really knows what to do or say in that situation? From talking to all my friends I have made over the last 10 years, I don't know anyone who felt like they dealt with their results day very well.

My feelings at this time were still stagnant; they hadn't really progressed from numbness. The only thing I knew was that our lives were about to turn upside down, life as we knew it was about to change and I didn't really know why.

At this stage, the only words I had heard were 'bone tumor': my mind had not related the words 'bone tumor' to cancer. As far as I can recall, I don't remember anyone using the word 'cancer'. Silly plum here thought, "It can't be that bad, it's only a bone tumor and it's probably fixable!"

The group of doctors then started talking about plan of action, what and when treatment would start. Whilst they were jabbering on, we all just sat in pure mental craziness. There were far too many doctors in that small room, it was stuffy and hot, they were all standing there gawping at us with solemn looks on their faces and we had no idea who they all were.  Although I do remember "Julie the Wonder Nurse" being there, who is the most fantastic nurse in the world and deserves to win an OBE of some kind. As for the rest of them, they gave me the same look as those doctors at my local hospital.... "Walking Dead!"  At the time I felt like saying, "what the fuck are you looking at me like that for!" but I knew my mother would smack my backside... lol. Looking back, those faces have really imprinted on me, it was as if they were saying.... "You've got no chance...!" Well I say, "Never underestimate a crazy teenager with the determination of a bull!"

Sitting in the appointment room my first question was, "When does all this treatment start then?" Briggsy replied, "Monday morning". Bear in mind this was a Thursday and my birthday, so I replied by saying, "let's put it off a week, I'm going on holiday tomorrow and have been saving for ages so I'm going." The look on my consultant (Briggs's) face was one I will never forget; he was shocked, amazed, inspired and had absolutely no idea what he was letting himself in for.

This Briggsy fella seemed to be the kind of consultant that got everything he wanted, walked on water and was treated like a God. However, he hadn't met me.  After I had decided a date to start my treatment, we talked about the plan of action. I do love a plan of action, and this was something that Briggsy was going to learn about me.

Briggsy explained that he was going to send me to see his very good friend and colleague, Mr. Jeremy Whelan, to start my chemotherapy (which was just a medicine to me), after which surgery would be decided on the rate of which the chemo…. medicine was working.  The enormity still hadn't sunk in….. Oh well.  This Jezza chap sounded nice, and it appeared that he knew what he was doing. From then on, we knew that we would be ok with these two hot shots in charge of us.

I've never really being comfortable with the whole Mr. and Professor titles, it kinda made me feel a little inferior, so right from word go I decided I would give my two guardian angels their own unique titles…. Briggsy and Jezza….. They've never said anything to me over the last 10 years and I still continue to call them by their nicknames to this date. They are like part of the family and we all have a little nickname.

After we talked everything through with the doctors and asked all the questions we needed to ask as a family, it was time to go home.  Though I cannot clearly remember any of the questions that we asked, I'm pretty sure if you were in our shoes you would have asked the same things we did. However, I do remember Briggsy telling me I was going to lose my hair, but it didn't bother me.  Apparently there was nothing I could do about it, so I decided I wasn't about to start worrying.

The journey home was very quiet, we all had thoughts about what was going to happen, I was sure there were things my parents weren't saying to me, and there were many things which I kept to myself.

However, when we got home it was back to business as usual. We had a massive Chinese takeaway, which consisted of special chow mien, special fried rice, spare ribs and prawn crackers. It was my birthday so we had a little bit of wine and got the party started. We were due to go on holiday the next day to centre parks. It was somewhere we had been for the last couple of years, and my folks took a group of us for the week. After dinner and wine, we packed for our holiday and really had a great night.

During my holiday, we had an amazing time. I did everything Briggsy told me not to do, e.g. and sports or heavy dancing... as if that was really going to happen!! In fact on one evening I told the DJ it was my 18th Birthday, and then he told the whole bar to buy me a drink. My mum says she watched me drink approx. 23 Smirnoff ice bottles. I'm not sure I actually finished them all, but it was wicked. From their point of view, I suppose they thought that this was the last chance I might actually get to enjoy myself, so they just watched and let me get on with it. *I think that night I had the best time ever so big hugs to James, Dan, Tom, Barry, Gemma and the best brother in the world.*

I didn't think about my bone tumor too much whilst away, though I did have a few conversations with my parents about fertility; that seemed to be something my mum was worried about. It felt as though they were trying to prepare me for what was about to come.....Oh how naive we were. Looking back, I still didn't really see the severity of the situation. I knew what was going to happen, however, I didn't think there was anything was wrong with that; being told you have a bone tumor in your leg and that that they are going to chop it out and shove a piece of metal in its place didn't seem to faze me.

My worries only came when I saw the looks on other people's faces when I told them what was wrong with me. They would cry, tell me how sorry they were for me, ask if there is anything they can do and quite frankly that was weird....... It felt like pity and I really don't do pity! I tried not to let it get to me, however there were a few occasions I felt like saying, "Get a grip! You're not the sick one here - do you see me crying?" I think most of them thought I was going to die, but I had other plans!

# 4 THE BEGINNING

Thoughts of treatment whirled through my mind every second of every day, right up the point we had to set off for my first day of chemo. I didn't know what to expect and to be honest I didn't want to think about it, as that meant it was more real. I knew what drugs they going to give me, but looking back I was still very naive to what was truly happening.

As shocking as it sounds, I made the decision to cut my hair short before I started chemo. I have always had long blonde luscious hair throughout my life, so cutting it short was going to be an interesting look for me.

Understanding I couldn't stop the process of my hair falling out didn't make me feel scared, afraid or nervous. Knowing I was going to be a baldy was kind of crazy but cool, and it saved on shampoo! ... All I could think was, "why worry about it?". It may sound strange but losing my hair didn't bother me that much; it was a very small part to the enormity of what was about to happen.

During this phase, the reality that my treatment was going to take up a lot of time really kicked in. I knew I had to give up college for a year and that my friends would go on to graduate without me. I was sad about this as I loved college and the hospital wasn't really going to help my social life. Anyway.... after I had the hair chop, I donated to my hair to my local college to allow students to practice colour and perm testing. This saved them cutting their own hair. I had the chance to buy some bandanas and headwear before I went to hospital in preparation for losing my hair completely, though looking back maybe I should have bought some wax to polish my upcoming slap top!

My dad took me to start my first chemo session. We took the train from Sittingbourne to London (it felt like it took forever) and when we got to London we jumped on the manic tube train for a short while. It was so busy in London and my leg was in agony as I had been over doing it on holiday. I think the worst part of the journey was finishing off with a small walk to the hospital, *which killed!* The journey was filled with uneasy and very fake conversation. Uncertainty occupied our minds. I'm sure my dad was petrified and I knew I had no idea what I was about to do.

At this stage I was in a lot of pain, I was struggling to walk, and as we approached our destination it all started to become more real. On our final stretch we prepared for our arrival at the Hospital: my heart raced a little, the suspense was overwhelming, my dad and I kept looking at each other and not really knowing what to say. I suppose that was kinda normal for a teenage girl and her dad.

When we got to the hospital, I couldn't believe how big the place was. Just looking at the wards map was completely overwhelming and my brain did that thing where it spiraled out of control as we paused looking at the map. When we finally found where the ward was on the map, we headed off in an up and left direction.... And there it was: the Teenage Cancer Trust Unit.

After arriving at our destination, we were shown to a bed by a nurse, told to make ourselves at home and were told someone will be with us shortly. OMG!!!! Now I'm not sure if it's possible to make yourself at home on a ward when everywhere you look you can see young people with no hair and very sad parents. We felt soooooo uncomfortable; I just wanted to get up and leave. Neither of us knew which way to look as we didn't want to offend anyone by staring. It was also really difficult to tell the boys and the girls apart; if anything, that frightened me more. What was I going to look like bald??? My dad was great - he supported me and kept my spirits high throughout our wait for the nurse to come over. If I remember rightly, I think we played a game of cards.

Finally.... a nurse came over to book me in and sorted us out. She introduced herself as Vicky and got started, "You can call me Mrs. Vicky, it's my nickname". She seemed so nice. It was explained to us that I would be having a Hickman line fitted that evening.... we had no idea what this was and where they were putting it: no pressure there then! However, another nurse approached us with a long tubey thing which had two heads on it; one green and one red. This was a Hickman line and they were putting it into my chest. *Oh thank god for that, for a minute there I thought they were going to shove it my arse!*

I asked if I had to have one and she explained that this is how they will be administering my chemo: apparently it saved them poking my with needles every day.  I was up for this, as I hate needles. Although my brother Brian is a diabetic and I see needles every day, when they are heading in my direction, I run!  One thing I found strange was that the nurses were talking to us like we knew what was going on. We looked like startled rabbits caught in some headlights. We were just bombarded with information and Hickman lines, chemo, tests and side effects. At one point, I wanted to ask her to stop while I made some notes as there was so much to take in. AHHHHHHHH!!!!!  To top it all off, and continuing on with her conversation, she explained it was all happening right away... OMG!

Food wasn't on the menu that day has they would be putting me under an anesthetic to put my Hickman line in, so by the afternoon I was starving, but kinda glad I had my last supper the night before... a proper home cooked meal! As the day progressed, both my dad and I were starting to settle in and beginning to relax, but before we knew it time had flown by and the porter had arrived to take me down to theatre.  One part of me was, "Cool lets go, I'm ready!", but the other part of me was saying, "Woah woah woah, what's going on here .... this is too fast, I don't even know what you're doing to me!! Ahhhhh!"

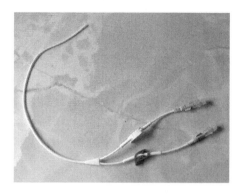

Only 2 hours later, I was back on the ward with a lovely white Hickman line hanging out of chest in between my bresticles. All that was left to do for that day was to test it out to ensure it was placed correctly, so Mrs. Vicky pressed start. I truly couldn't believe how fast everything was moving: it was like we had only just arrived and they had cut me open, shoved some tubes in my chest and had so many different people poking and prodding me. My head was bursting with what could only be described as the alphabet in a washing machine... no real words or thoughts, just everything in super drive. After this crazy whirlwind, I was ready for bed! That night the nurses ran saline through my line to ensure it was placed properly and I also had a chest X-Ray so the doctors could make sure it wasn't too close to my heart, which was very important.

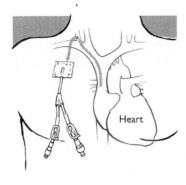

Heart

*Sleep time….* As I awoke for the next day, a strategic timetable of tests was upon me. Now, I thought I'd just have one or two but I was wrong… I was tested from every angle, I had kidney function test, liver function test, hearing test, sight test, full blood count and to finish off the day, a Muga heart scan. I have to say it was a little overwhelming as my dad and I had to travel over London to different hospitals, as years ago the UCLH was scattered all over London's city centre. Oh, and yes they did provide us with a hospital car to drive from place to place; I could just see us know jumping on the tube with my tubes hanging out lol!

The test results were due the next day and as far as I am aware they all came back ok, and the doctors were happy to start my chemo that night. Toward the end of the day, my dad and I had a chance to chill out and wait for tea. Now I'm not going to comment on how bad the food was; let's face it, hospital food has a little bit of a bad reputation. After talking with a few of the other parents, my dad had decided that as he was in the centre of London, he could pretty much get me anything I fancied. I sent him out to find me something nice and for tea that night we had an amazing lasagne, fresh from a little restaurant just around the corner from the hospital.

My doctors had asked me if I would be willing to trial a new combination of chemo drugs. I wasn't sure if they were asking because they didn't know if it would work and I was a lab rat, or if they knew it would be a better combination and have more impact on the tumor. Either way, what did I have to lose? After discussing what the drugs were and what they would do to my body, my folks turned to me and said, "it's your decision!" and that was it, the plan was set my D.I.M.E would start in the morning. I have to say that whole conversation was like an out of body experience... I didn't really get what was going on. We were whisked into this room and given a mountain of information which may determine the effectiveness of my treatment...... Wow.... My folks looked happy with it so I suppose that kinda swayed my decision.

My dad and I were relaxing for the evening just chatting and watching a bit of tele when Mrs. Vicky walked toward me. She had a tray with all sorts of tubes, syringes, bags of saline and a couple of brightly coloured bags that looked a little like lucozade. *How wrong was I, this was it, ahhhhhhhhh.*

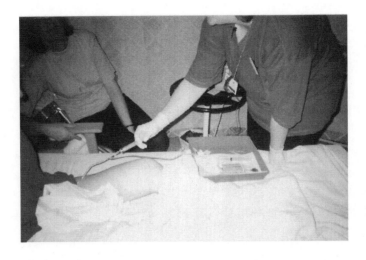

That night they put up my first round of chemo bags. I was very observant as she was connecting my lines. I watched as she used sterile utensils to prep her area and then it began. She started by pushing a small amount of saline through my tubes just to make sure they weren't blocked. It was cold in my chest and I could feel the saline as it ran through my veins. Then she drew back; that was the disgusting bit as I saw my blood flow back into the syringe... ewww.

Once both lines were clear, she started to connect drugs. I watched the poison as it flowed through the drip stand and into my new and ready tested Hickman line. The fear and anxiety was indescribable, I can't begin to try and explain it, I just felt like I was going to burst. Within minutes I felt sick, but I knew this was just in my head.... for now. The nurse told me to "try and get some sleep". However, all I could do was watch my chemo drip through the machine; my eyes were fixed, it was mesmerising, *no need for counting sheep!* I must have drifted off to sleep at some stage, as when I woke up

in the morning I puked my guts up silly!! And there it was.....
*The beginning.*


My family and I had all entered a world of science, drugs and all things medical. We were about to become experts in all things related to chemo, Hickman lines, sterilisation, blood counts and tumor related stuff. I got a D in science, so this world seemed impossible to grasp and there was so much to remember. During this time, there were no chances to get anything wrong, we had to do it right or I could get ill....
OMG


That first morning when I woke, my body felt strange: it was like I had been mixing my drinks the night before. Now was the time I had to learn how to take tablets, as this was something I had always struggled with all my life, and I was about to learn this very painfully and very quickly. As a child my mum would always give me Calpol, as I refused to even try tablets. So, when Mrs. Vicky brought me my first lot of pills I almost cried, I traumatically cut the tablets into a million pieces, whilst my head and heart were saying... "I'm not swallowing them!" It usually took me a couple of hours to take one set of pills and by the time I had finished them, she was back with more. I hated it; I found it the most stressful thing about my treatment, and I know to the average person tablets are easy, but my throat just didn't want to play! At one point I couldn't walk in a straight line, so Mrs. Vicky brought me some more little tablets, which were anti-sickness. I needed these to keep me on my feet, stop my head from spinning and keep as much food down as possible. Sadly for my dad, that lovely lasagne didn't look so lovely coming back up! That morning... it was like I had changed, I was a different person, I was strong, determined and ready to fight, I just wish I knew why I was fighting. Over my treatment, this process of taking tablets got easier but there were some that I just couldn't swallow, so they ended up giving them to me intravenously.... Up my Hickman line!... Thank god!

My chemotherapy was based on a cycle of 4 weeks: week one was Doxorubicin, Etopside and Ifosfamide every night for 4 nights in a row and then home for a bit to rest; on the beginning of week 3 I had one bag of Methotrexate followed by 72 hours of saline flushing. You couldn't go home with this particular drug still in your system, not sure exactly why but I think it was to do with how toxic it was. By then we were back round to start all over again with week one. This concoction was tailored by the lovely Jezza; he has a little more grey hair now, but don't tell him I said that!

It wasn't an exact science, as there were a few cycles which were longer and some shorter, but we had a plan and it was a good one!

We had learned that the drugs had different side effects for different people. For example, the first time my Methotrexate was administered, I had what could only be described as an allergic reaction. From this, my body resisted the drug and it caused me to have a seizure during the night. The doctors and nurses were on hand to give me counteraction drugs and apparently it slowly wore off. I don't really remember much about that night, apart from the pain I was getting in my nervous system; it was all over my body, like a burning sensation running through my veins, it was agony.

By morning, though tired, I was much better. The burning pain was only in the palms of my hands and the soles of feet, which was being helped by more drugs. My dad was by my side all night; it must have been so scary for him to watch his only daughter have several seizures throughout the night. *My dad is Superdad.* The morning before my seizure, I shaved my hair off as it was falling out and getting all knotted. It didn't bother me as I knew it was falling out, so I thought, "what the hell, let's go skin head"! However, overnight whilst my head was thrashing all over the place, my dad explained that he had to changed my pillow case 3 times as it was covered in short stubby hair, and by morning the back of my head was completely bald. I looked so funny. A sideways monk....

Coincidently, the morning after my seizure, the wig lady came to fit me with some luscious locks. *It was the funniest thing;* I went into the room bald and came out with shoulder length hair. I couldn't help myself, I took one look at a new patient called Ross and said, "they don't tell you how quick it'll grow back!" With a swish of my new locks and scowling look from him, I turned around and whipped it off rather quickly. I don't think he was very impressed. Mind you, from that day we become besy mates; it turned out we were on the same chemo, and had the same tumor, we also ended up having our surgery at the same time, so we spent a lot of time together.

# 5 WARD LIFE

Mentally, I spent a lot of time just being very tired and not thinking too much. Some of my friends really struggled with their emotions and to be honest I never truly understood some of their approaches toward their treatment. I saw some teens blame their parents for their cancer, some just stopped talking altogether but I was more.... Gung-ho.... bull in a china shop. I never really knew why, I just found it easier to know everything that was going on with me and then that way there were no questions.

Being on a ward full sick people when you don't feel like a sick person is really strange. When I woke in the mornings, it would take me some time to get through my regime of peeing in a pot, washing my armpits, cleaning my teeth, using the most disgusting mouthwash and then the pills.... However there were others that insisted in staying in bed all day, not even putting clothes on. I found this strange, but everyone had their own way of dealing with everything that was going on. I took it upon myself to cheer anyone up who needed it. To be honest, I didn't stop to think why I was like that, why I was sorting everyone else out before myself. We played word games across the ward when we couldn't get out of bed and watched films when we needed to be quiet. I think my folks led the way and I just followed. My mum and Debbie would have 11 teens when they were in together and if anyone needed anything they would be there. Some parents couldn't be in everyday so they looked after everyone.

A massive side effect from chemo was either major weight loss or weight gain due to steroids. Not really sure which I would have preferred, however mine was the first. I lost super weight... my poor mother, bless her.

When I started my treatment, she was trying to encourage me to eat really healthy foods so I was getting the right nutrients, vitamins and minerals. Any sane person would have done the same thing. I don't think I had ever eaten so much veg! Approximately 3 weeks into my treatment during a regular weigh-in session, Mrs. Vicky was disappointed as I had lost a significant amount of weight: I had gone from 9 ½ stone to 7 and looked very pale and gaunt. She took the decision to send the dietician round to see us and work out why I had lost so much weight so quickly. When she arrived, my mum looked very nervous; she explained she had been feeding me healthy food and couldn't understand my weight loss. The dieticians response was, "she needs to eat junk food to keep the fat on!" My mum was horrified as she had always engrained into me to be healthy as a child and now it's all junk food and chocolates! Oh dear!. *"Yay, chocolate for breakfast, lunch and dinner!"* Well that's what

I thought anyway, but that didn't happen. As time went on throughout my treatment, my taste buds went crazy. I liked things I had disliked before, but I still loved all my favourites, like chocolate and pastries. My mum had to give in to my temptation and let me have whatever I fancied. At the start it was hard, but with a strong team effort I believe we had a system going. If I managed to eat something for breakfast, then that meant I would manage a few things throughout the day.

A typical meal plan consisted of an apple for breakfast, some toast or a sandwich for lunch and for tea. It was always as much as I could eat throughout the day but chocolate was my favourite snack. However, if I couldn't do breakfast, my folks knew they had a battle on their hands as my lips were sealed for the day. It seemed like everything I ate came back up at some stage, so what was the point of putting anything in me. I remember being at home for a night and my dad said, "Let's have a Chinese". My eyes lit up (he knew I love Chinese), I piled my plate high and stuffed my face…. I think it took approx. 15 mins for my whole dinner to come back up again.

Now, if I had been on the vodka all night I wouldn't have felt so bad, but I did, and apologised all night.

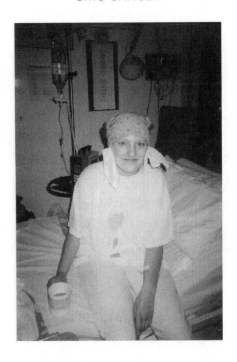

For me, the sicknesses started right from word go but really started to kick in about 2 weeks into my treatment. It started with constant nausea and progressed to a complete loss of appetite, and every time there was a strong aroma I was sick.  Baked Beans were my nemesis: every time I tried to eat them, they just came flowing back up. They were quite an easy transaction really and I loved the flavour, so that was the only thing I didn't mind vomiting back up.  I have always loved my food and it became more difficult for me to eat. I knew I had to but I didn't want to: knowing everything I put into my mouth it was coming straight back up started to become mentally hard.  It was that bad that if visitors ever brought flowers to the ward, my mum and the nurses would have to check and see if there were Lilies in the bunch, as the mere smell would make many of us extremely nauseous. My mum would sneak round to their flowers and take out the pollen strands, as that's the part that smelled.... It's disgusting! Even to this day, whenever I smell Lilies it makes me feel sick, think of cancer sickness and balding.

You would think that having cancer was the hardest part, but you would be wrong. It's the side effects that really get you. Looking back now, I can't believe how much of our time was spent worrying about how much food I had eaten, how much food I had then vomited up, what my fluid intake was and how many times I had weeeed that day. These were the first and last questions of the day and pretty much a constant throughout. There were days I felt a little nagged by my folks and Mrs. Vicky, but underneath I knew it was for my own good.

My mum always made me take a walk to the little shop in the hospital, as it was important for me to get out of bed and get some exercise from time to time and it was important to not let other patients get me down. There were times where some patients were having a real downer day, and getting out of the ward was vital to both mine and my mum's mental state. We must have looked really bonkers; there was me in my baggy clothes that no longer fitted due to my weight loss, a drip stand with chemo running through, slippers, bald head probably bearing a funky hat or bandana, a box of tissues, crutches and a sick bucket! Poor shopkeeper! We generally bought chocolate, as this is what I pretty much lived on for a while. My mum and me were and still are very close, we have always had a good relationship: she picked me up when I was down and laughed with me when I was happy. I have to be honest, both my mum and dad knew how I was feeling all the time. When I needed to sleep, they let me and when I needed to be out of my bed they made it happen.

It's funny, after talking with my folks about our experiences, the realisation that our memories were so different was a little bit strange. I suppose I was in the moment and never really saw it as they did.  They used to talk about how difficult I was when it came to getting me to eat, and all I remember is eating loads and being sick loads. However, thankfully they constantly persevered.

Making friends is hard in that place but we did it. It was nice to have friends in hospital, it kinda made the experience more normal; well as normal as normal could be.  I was 17, bald and had a massive tumor growing in my leg...hmmm.... Maybe not physically normal, but the conversation was much better than with my folks all day every day. I know my mum is fab company, she is as crazy as me, but having people my own age was amazing.  When you felt like shit and needed someone to talk to you could talk to your mates as they understood. At times you didn't want to burden your parents; let's face it they were dealing with some hard emotions themselves as they watch their child suffer in pain, *that's gotta be difficult.*

Chemotherapy is hard; it's like being on a rollercoaster and not knowing what's round each corner. I would like to say each day was different, but it was more like each hour.  As treatment went on, I learnt how to listen to my body.

When the sickness was coming I could prepare myself, when I was starting to get dizzy I knew I had to be on my bed and as soon as the pain set in it was important to get relief asap. For someone like me who loves a plan of action, I had to learn that planning was never going to work in this situation, I

37

spent a lot of time saying, "I'll see how I feel!" I think my mum and dad were good at keeping me going and keeping up with my ever-changing problems... I don't think my mum went anywhere without a sick bucket, tissues or pills!

As I got used to the chemo (well, as much as anyone could get used to chemo), I found it easier to cope with the symptoms, and as strange as it seems, being sick just became natural and I ate food to ensure that I could puke something up.... Haha...Something was better than nothing.... Trust me, when that bile burns the back of throat.... you learn very quickly.....

My treatment spanned over a year and during that time, I made some amazing friends; Aaron, Ross, Matt, Claire and Gary were the guys I generally saw when chemo was due.

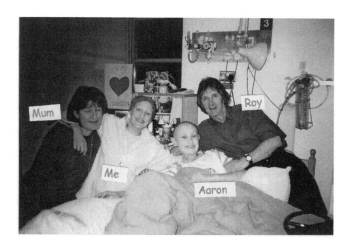

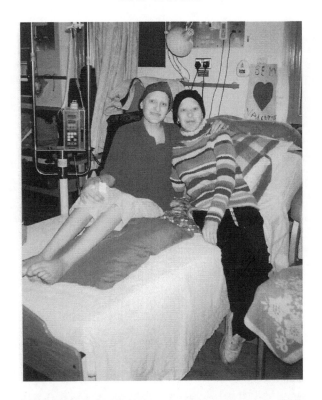

Seeing familiar faces made treatment so much easier. It was a relief to see someone you knew when you walked on the ward. There were some occasions when there were no people I knew on the ward, which made it difficult.

I remember a talk that Ross and I had; we were sat in the day room, our mums had set us up with tissues, drinks and a sick bucket each to watch some tele while they went for a walk to get fresh air. Ross sat there and said, "Caz this cancer stuff it's shit, I don't get it?!" He had tears in his eyes. I paused to think how to respond, but when I paused.... It just clicked: for the first time, I had realised that Ross and I had the same thing, so that meant I had cancer. No one had ever said 'cancer' to me; they only said 'bone tumor', but for that moment I tried to forget my thoughts to console him; I grabbed him and squished him.

We talked for a while about how crap we felt and how the drugs were making us feel. I think it made him feel better as he wasn't one to show emotions, but in that moment I believe we both needed it. I was glad he didn't mention death, as I'm pretty sure I wouldn't have dealt with that conversation very well. I daren't mention the fact my brain was running round in circles from the revelation I had just had. I had just started cycle 2 and for the first time I had put the pieces together. "Wow.... OMG....Ahh" were just a few of the feelings I had whilst Ross and I watched TV that afternoon. I was so glad when our mums got back, as my head was about ready to explode. Funnily enough, I never really mentioned our chat to anyone, I felt like it was between us and Ross just really needed a friend.

Though there were opportunities to meet new patients, I found a really good friend in Ross. From the day we met we were like the two musketeers; we were on the same treatment so it was nice to be able to talk about how the chemo made us feel. Funnily enough, when we had the Doxorubicin/Etopside/Ifosfamide part of the cycle, I puked my guts silly but Ross was fine, and the when we had the Methotrexate part I was fine and Ross puked silly instead. It was comforting to know we were not alone. We always laughed about our side effects and poop was always top topic. I think Ross just used to treat me like one of the boys.... lol, well I was bald and looked very similar to my brother without the hair!!! I didn't mind though. We shared a lot of experiences together throughout our treatment, with chemo and surgery, and I had always hoped we would stay in touch when we finished our doing our time.

Thankfully, Ross managed to put up with me.... we would chat on the phone nearly every other week, and sometimes for a good hour or so. Although during one phone call, Ross sounded a little nervous. We normally just talked about life, college, work, girls for him, boys for me.... oh and his cars.

However, this time was different. He started talking about a pain in his chest, then threw in the fact he had got engaged with his lady friend (sorry I've forgot her name!)... OMG... then went back to his pain in his chest.... Hmmm... I stopped him and said, "Is everything ok??" he replied with "No!" and went on to tell me that he had relapsed recently, but didn't say anything as he didn't want to worry me..... Not worry.... Shit... this had to be bad... He said, "they're not going to give me anything..... do you understand what that means...?" Shit... it was really bad, I just said, "Yeah.... I know...!" and that was the last conversation I had with him. Shortly after, he became very poorly and couldn't really do anything. I wished I lived closer to him, I would have been there every day if possible. I often think Ross and I were so good friends because there was no need to say anything, we both understood how we felt inside and out, as we had been through the same thing and felt the same pain.

When I lost Ross, I was so angry at the world, I wanted to shout at the doctors for not doing enough, and I wanted to know why they let this happen to him. I went to Ross's funeral and I felt so sad, though I didn't want to cry, because I know Ross would have hated that! My dad cried, and I believe it was about relief, as that could have been his daughter. It might sound strange but I've kept the last crimbo card that Ross sent me, as it is something to remember him by. I generally stick it on the mantelpiece at crimbo.... Some people just need to be remembered.

# 6 MY ON-GOING ADVENTURES WITH SUSIE

Many of the teenage cancer trust units have a person who works as an activities co-ordinator; this is a person who motivates you during the day to try to get you out of bed. From just watching a DVD in the day room to being creative with some art work, their job also consisted of a lot of talking with patients, as there will be days where getting out of bed is just not possible. Having someone to communicate with who does not feel sorry for you or stare at your bald head is quite comforting.

When I first arrived on the unit it was quite scary, and I was not sure if the person in the next bed was a girl or a boy. I did not want to ask and look a plum, so I politely introduced myself and a very gentle voice replied, "Is it your first day?" "Don't worry, you'll get the hang of this place soon enough, if you need anything, just ask. I know what my first day was like!", which made me feel at ease. After a few days into my treatment, this lady came up to me and said, "Hi my name is Susie, I'm quite new here, but I am the activities co-ordinator for this unit." She sat herself on my bed and we started to chat, just about random stuff, nothing important like the fact I was just about to start my chemotherapy and was bricking it, but we talked about music, TV and the outside world. From that day, I felt as though I could call Susie my friend, she was there for both me and my folks when we needed it.

Susie and I had many adventures whilst I was on the unit. On the days I could get out of bed, she would get me doing activities. She loved getting messy and turning the ward into Picasso's art gallery, we painted many murals using the pool table as our work station,

it was situated smack bang in the middle of the unit so it was perfect for a table!! We never really put the art work up, but we had a great time doing it. I didn't even realise that I had my chemo running through, it was a great distraction.

One of my favourite experiences with Susie was when she turned up in the morning at 9am with a bag full of ingredients, sat on my bed and said, "Today we are Jamie Oliver and we going bake a cake." Now this was hilarious, as we all knew Susie had no idea how to cook, let alone bake a cake. We were in stitches when she then pulls out a book and said, "look I've even got a cook book to follow!!" It was an offer I couldn't pass up, so I got myself dressed and we took a slow walk to the kitchen. I say slow walk, we had to use the children's ward's kitchen, which was at the other side of the hospital, as our kitchen had just enough room for one person to make a cuppa but that was it.

We started by getting all the ingredients out and ready. Susie was in charge of the cookbook, which was a little dangerous, however I thought it would be worse if she had control of the mixer. There was a point where she tried to mix some flour in, and OMG she had a little trouble with the mixing spatula. She just couldn't get circular motion in her wrists and my mum was laughing her head off saying, "come on Susie flick those wrists!" She looked so keggy handed it was funny as hell, she was shouting, "I can't mix this, it's too hard, don't tell anyone they'll laugh at me!!" Ha ha ha ha ha! On the up-side when the cake came out of the oven, it was great. I couldn't believe how nice it tasted. We shared it around the ward to both patients and nurses, and thankfully no one was sick.

I think Susie liked to practice her cooking on the ward. She would arrange cooking competitions for patients and parents; she called it the 'mystery ingredient cook off'.....
One time we got a papaya and octopus in a tin, I mean what the hell were we supposed to do with that lol! My brother is a chef and he was stumped, so we had no hope of winning that one.

Now our Susie could talk the hind legs off a donkey, and she spent a lot of time on the phone organising "stuff for you guys!" as she called it. However, when you watched Susie on the phone you could see her getting slightly bored of many conversations and there was a key word you had to listen out for, this was 'FANTASTIC'. It was said in slow motion, but this meant she had lost all interest and had absolutely no idea what she had just agreed to. On one particular day, I was in isolation as I had had a nose bleed for 1 ½ hours in the car ride to the hospital and I had to wait for some blood before I started my chemo. I thought I would be super bored waiting for my blood. However, a very excitable Gary came zooming onto the ward laughing his head off saying, "We're all getting pissed tonight!!" He explained there was a massive trolley carrying 4 or 5 crates of Virgin booze coming our way. Now chemo and booze may not be the best idea, but we thought 'what the hell'.


At that time, the nurses were having change over so the ward was a little empty apart from the patients and parents, and this very tall dark and handsome chap rolled his trolley onto the ward and we were all thinking... what has Susie done now? Gary's mum Jan went to fetch Susie out of the staff room to sort out the chap and his trolley. It transpired that whilst she was on the phone that morning she had agreed for what she thought was 600 cans of Virgin Cola, this turned out to be 300 bottles of Virgin NT (with vodka), 200 cans of Virgin DT Energy drink (without vodka) and only 30 cans of Virgin Cola.

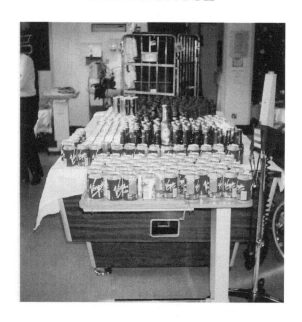

Now where did she go wrong...hmmmm... I think it was when she said "fan-tas-tic" (with a little nodding dog action). The laughing started when he continued to say, "I need the trolley and crates back so I have to empty them now". Well, where do you put all those cans and bottles? The mums took action and they started by filling the bottom drawers in all the cabinets by our beds, they then filled the pool table, the fridge in the both the nurses room and our kitchen and they used a few trolley tables to finish off. After it was all unloaded, we were all in hysterics, Ross and I were playing cards whilst the others were playing eye spy across the ward, when one of the nurses came up to us and said Dr Jezza (Dr Jeremy Whelan) is doing a ward round shortly and the booze needs to be moved.

OMG there were frantic black bags flying all over the place and all the mums were running around the ward like headless chickens trying to make the place ready for the doctors ward round. We were all sat together and when Dr Jezza arrived, it was hard to contain the giggles. Of course then the eye spy game got a little out of hand when someone suggested F for fridge, which was then swiftly followed by FF for full fridge. We were howling with laughter and Jezza had no idea. We all figured that as we had already had our blood tested in the morning it would be alright for us to crack open a few bottles while Jezza was doing his ward round, we were all slurping alcopops in plastic cups.... I don't think I've laughed so hard during my treatment but that day was the best.

Susie has a magic about her, she would made you feel better every day, it did not matter that you looked like crap and felt a million times worst, she just brightened your day to the point that there were times I did not realise chemo was running through my veins. Her work on the unit made such a difference to so many people, not just me, but all the patients. I feel like she is a big part to my survival and I will be in debt to her indefinitely.

My relationship with Susie today is great. Even now she is there for me when I need to talk to someone who understands. We have been through weddings, funerals, more weddings and crazy lives. She is still working for the TCT, however now she is in the education team spreading the work in local schools, making sure the teenagers of today are aware that cancer can affect them in many ways. From all accounts, I've been told that she is fab when she gets up in front of the teens and does her thing! I am so proud of her ongoing work and dedication to the charity.


Oh and I promised I would not mention her sexy black PVC cat suit that she wore whilst growling provocatively at a photographer during her sexy photo shoot...... She mentioned something about killing me, but I can't quite remember her exact words lol!!!!  Love ya Susie X

# 7 SURGERY TIME

The prospect of having my bones hacked, sawed then chopped up with utensils you would normally find in the butchers was surprisingly not appealing, and gladly they informed me, I would not have to watch. Mentally, going into surgery felt a little numb as knowing the only other option was to chop my leg off, having the prostheses put in to replace the half of my femur and my knee seemed like the best option.

I think for the first time in my life, I was glad to be 17 as this meant that my mum could stay on the hospital grounds with me and be with me every day. I think just knowing she would be there for me when I woke up was a relief, mind you I think I may have used her as my verbal pain punching bag from time to time!! Sorry Mum!! By this stage during my treatment, my family and I were getting used to the hospital lingo and living out of suitcases. In a way, we were ready for anything and happy to go along with whatever Briggsy and Jezza suggested.

Though the surgery sounded a little drastic, we agreed no questions asked as to how and why. I can't believe someone as inquisitive as me didn't question Briggsy's judgment. This man was about to chop my leg open and I was about to let him. I think that we all loved Briggsy so much by that stage anything would go. My surgery took place at a different hospital as Briggsy (Proff. Tim Briggs) my surgeon and his team were based all over the place.

My experience at The Royal National Orthopaedic Hospital was different. The hospital did not have a teenage ward so being 17 I was classed as a child and put on the children's ward where babies were set like a timer to cry every evening at 8pm, 9pm and then 10pm like clockwork, mind you I could give them a run for their money lol. The only plus side to this ward was that my mum could stay with me.

Apparently this was what they were about to put inside me....... OOoooo Shiny... I wasn't really sure how I feel about that, but there were no other options. Today my metal work is getting a little rusty, maybe a little painful and if you listen to my husband he'll tell you that I generally ignore the pain, so as to not miss out on anything. I have had a couple of M.O.T operations but I have been told that it has a lifetime guarantee and the repairs are free so I can have as many as I want! Briggsy once said to me, "If you break it, I'll fix it, don't worry!" I'll hold him to that!

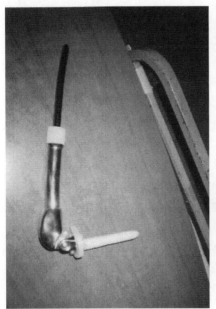 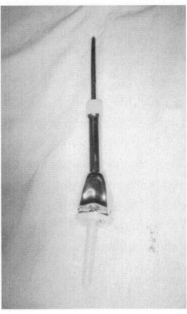

Monday 23rd October 2000 at 9am was chop day and the night before was a restless one. My mum and I were not sure what to expect, and I am glad we did not know what was coming or we may have given it a miss. When the nurse woke me up to get me into my sexy gown and paper pants that meant the porters were on their way to take me down to surgery and we were about to venture into the unknown. My heart raced ten to the dozen. I was still suffering a little from my last chemo round, so going into surgery I wasn't feeling 100%. Tired, bald and looking like crap pretty much summed up how I felt and looked. I think my mum was petrified though she would never say. She just tried to stay strong for me. Looking back now I can see where I get my strength from, I don't think I could have got through any of it without the strength of my family.

All dressed and ready, looking sexy, my mum walked down to the anaesthetic room with me and was able to stay while they knocked me out, but she then had to go back to the ward to wait it out. I can't imagine how that must have felt for my mum; watching your child be put to sleep has to be terrifying. My heart raced until they pushed that magic white potion through my Hickman line and I started to count down from 10. I can't say what happened during surgery as I was asleep, but I can safely say when I woke up I felt like death. There was a rule that all children's ward patients spent the night on the ICU (intensive care unit) to help them re-adjust after surgery. I think I slept there for several days. When I finally woke, I was puking up grey creamy stuff and the pain was very interesting. I thought I was meant to have pain in my leg, however there seemed to be a very bad pain in my tummy and due to the epidural I really shouldn't have been able to feel anything from the waist down. For some reason this crippling in pain was so intense. I could see the worry on the nurses faces, and after a quick investigation on my downstairs area the nurse decided that my bladder was about to burst, seriously she had to move fast! So she swiftly shoved a catheter up my pee pee hole and had the fright of her life, as I very quickly filled 2 pee bags which overflowed as she tried to change them. Bless her, she did make a mess on the floor! I remember her saying, "surely that's not possible" as she popped her head up and looked at me. It felt strange not being able to feel anything but shortly after my bladder had finished emptying the pain subsided, thankfully! After I had fully recovered from the shock of surgery I was transferred back to the children's unit where the nurses were glad to see me.

As I was the only patient with a Hickman line on the ward, I realised that they were not as common as first thought and many of the nurses were not trained to administer drugs through it. Now by this stage in my treatment, I could take my own blood out of my line and administer antibiotics myself, though at that time they wouldn't let me; I was just out of surgery after all. Subsequently the nurses used me as an opportunity to get their Hickman line qualification. I felt honoured that I could help them, mind you being woken at 2am in the morning to a giggly excitable nurse who was nervous and wanting to give me some drugs, was a little tedious every night but I was happy to help.

A few days after surgery I begin my physiotherapy which started out ok, however when my epidural came out it started to become unbearably painful and the progress was very slow. My leg was strapped to a massive knee bending contraption which took over my whole bed and stuck my leg in the air, I hated it. I almost felt like a prisoner on my own bed, I couldn't move! When a week had passed unfortunately Briggsy and my physiotherapist were not happy with the progress I was making. Whenever I tried to bend my knee, I was getting an excruciating sharp pain in my knee joint. It was as if I was being stabbed with a hot, metal poky thing, however this transpired to be scar tissue developing within my knee joint...... typical! And it was preventing my leg from bending properly. The only way to resolve this problem was for Briggsy to knock me out again and break the scar tissue that was building up. He had to do it by hand with a little brute force and elbow grease, or WD40..... can you imagine the bruises, they reached from hip to toe.

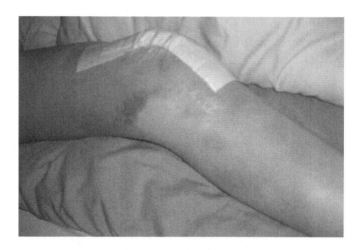

There was a lot of uncertainty between my mum and I, but the nurses told us that it is tremendously painful trying to break the scar tissue whilst I was awake, so back down to theatre I went for a leg breaking session. OMG what next....this had to be the most stressful part of my visit it the Royal National, I was completely at their mercy, I couldn't leave and I didn't want to stay! Before I woke from the second surgery, I was put on the knee bending machine so when my eyes opened all I could see was my leg going back and forth in a knees to chest action. OUCH... *why me!*

Having to get out of bed for the first time was really scary, my mind was full of anxiety and fear, as I thought my leg was going to pop open or break into two. Unfortunately I had no choice, this was it, I dare not put full weight on my leg, but a little was better than nothing. My heart raced, my palms were sweaty and my head was leg exploded with pain with each and every moment.

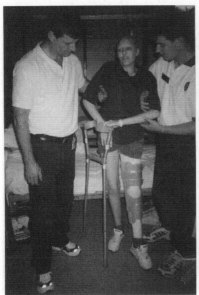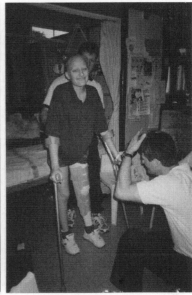

Physiotherapy became very tiresome, as I was putting in a lot of effort and not getting very far. The doctors explained I had to get my knee to bend at a 90 degree angle before they would let me leave the hospital, and from then on I was on a mission, mind you all I wanted to do was sleep. I think being a teenager made it difficult for the nurses as I had my own mind and I was very stubborn. Unlike some of the other children who would do as they were told, I tended to decide when I wanted to do physio and not when they wanted me to. Perhaps had I listened when told me to do my physio, maybe the leg breaking session could have been avoided lol.

After a few days, I started to feel unwell in the tummy and bottom region, which apparently explained a lot of the lethargy I was experiencing. Now when you've just had major surgery and can't walk, the last thing you need is a tummy problem, trust me. Overnight my condition worsened very quickly and the nurses felt I needed to have some tests done. I think I may have kept the whole ward up that night with my agonising tummy screams. I always worked on the basis that if I was hurting they would know about it, so I screamed a lot! When the results came back they found out I had contracted the deadly bug Clostridium Difficile, C-Diff for short, this was not a good thing. C-Diff is a bacterial infection causing diarrhoea, fever and stomach cramps, to any normal person the infection would have been reasonably easy to cure but I had no immune system from the chemo so I was at super risk. How did that happen? I hardly ever left my bed, why oh why did I have all the bad luck! I was put on very strong antibiotics straight away, on a wing and a prayer all we could do was wait, and of course do my knee bending physiotherapy Booo...! I had not realised that there were other drugs out there in the world of medicine that could make me feel just as bad as chemo. I thought I was there for a break from drugs, no such luck.

Looking back now, I didn't know that the C-Diff bug was deadly enough to finish me off at the time. I had no immune system, so the doctors and nurse were lucky to catch it quick before it took over my body..... I mean, to battle cancer and then trip at the last hurdle on a little bug.... That wouldn't have been good....PHEW!!!!

My physiotherapy sessions were still not going as well as I would have liked. The chap who was supposed to be looking after me didn't have the first idea of how to talk to a bald, frustrated, in pain teenage female. Our relationship was a little fragile; I shouted at him, he looked at me blankly, hence I shouted at him more. We just didn't click and it is important to get positive feedback when you have to do something which causes you so much pain. He gave me nothing and I pretty much hated him at the time. Obviously now that's different as I am a mature adult and would never hold a grudge. Over the next few days, the nurses picked up my negative attitude toward going to physio, and without telling me they had arranged to have a lady called Sarah to be my new physiotherapist. It was a lovely surprise when I turned up at my session and there was a beaming smile on her face, she welcomed me and my mum and made me feel special. I was so happy and my progression came on leaps and bounds, my 90 degree angle was coming on very well at this stage. It felt like she believed in me, and that was all I needed to push myself to reach my goal.

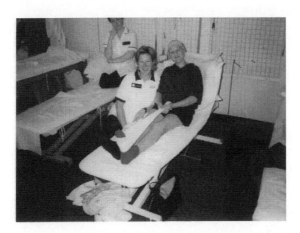

Whilst I was at the Royal National, Ross arrived to have his surgery. It was great to see him, and I gave him some words of wisdom and popped to see him every now and again on my way back from physio. As Ross was 18, he had to go on the adult ward with all the old men, which he hated. He said they used to stare at him because he was bald, and it also meant that his mum couldn't stay on the hospital grounds: as Ross was classed as an adult, he wasn't allowed anyone to stay with him. My mum popped to see him every day when his mum Debbie couldn't get in. We were all furious that she couldn't stop with my mum, but apparently "rules are rules." I have to say it was really nice to be able to see a friendly face: what with being stuck in that place for longer than needed, I was going stir crazy with boredom. I love my mum but seeing Ross was like a home from home, he was my hospital bessy mate and it had been ages since we chatted.

After week 3 at the Royal National, I had realised that I should really be getting back to my chemo so I asked the nurse why I hadn't gone yet and she said, "Well Caroline, you're contagious, so they've said we've gotta keep ya for a bit!... that ok??" Oh great..... When you're on chemotherapy your immune system is naff and supper low so bugs are really easy to catch... der.... and they didn't want me to spread my wealth. When week 4 started I was getting bored, I could just about do the painful knee bend, and although I wasn't completely bearing weight on my leg, I could whiz around on my crutches perfectly fine and my feet were going exactly where I was telling them to.

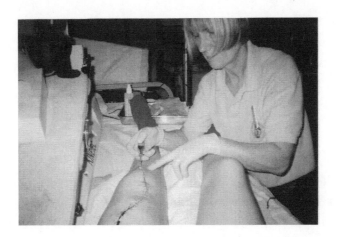

I continued to do my physio and pushed myself as hard as I could, and because I was in the hospital longer than a usual patient, I was able to have my staples taken out whilst I was there and have a go in the hydrotherapy pool. This helped me get used to my leg without bearing any weight... it was so lovely and warm! Physio seemed to be the first and last thing I thought about every day, five times a day, up to 45 mins a time and hydro 3-4- times a week. It kept me busy, as the rest of the time I was sleeping.

I wanted to get out of there so badly, both my mum and I were going mad. Until one morning; when I woke up I was looking a little pale and peaky and the nurses beeped the Dr several times to come and take my blood as they were a bit concerned the antibiotics were doing something they shouldn't.

However, it would seem he was rather busy and didn't have the time.....naughty man.... with his feet up!! Whilst I was watching TV that afternoon I had a visitor: Jezza (Mr. Jeremy Whelan) had walked himself onto the ward, past the nurse's station, found my bed, walked round it, pulled my eye lid and said, "You need blood!" No "hi, hello, how did the surgery go"... Nope, just the blood. After which, a nurse came running over saying, "May I ask who you are?" Bless her, she had no idea she was talking to my guardian angel... he responded by saying, "Yes of course, I am Mr. Jeremy Whelan Oncologist Consultant at the Middlesex Hospital London and this young lady needs blood, have you tested it?" My thoughts were, 'you're in trouble now'! The nurse explained she had been beeping the Dr all morning, but had no response. Jezza decided he would ring him himself whilst he was there and funnily enough he was on the ward in 2 minutes flat, which I believe was a record. It turned out that my blood level was extremely low and 3 bags of blood were needed. If he had waited any longer, I would have been a bad way. Once again, my guardian angel saved the day. Jezza didn't stay for long, he was just checking up on me and once he was happy he set off on his way. He did eventually ask about my surgery, which was cool.

At the end of week 4, we were about ready for the great escape, we had a plan that I would slip out the back while no one was looking…. It didn't work, I couldn't move fast enough! After some careful decision-making, Briggsy and Jezza let me go home for a week to spend some time with my family and have a break from all the drugs. My hair even started to grow a little bit and we dyed it electric blue, it was great.

You know, to this day I'm still not sure how I feel about having metal bones. It just feels like my left leg is a little slower than my right. Back then, I thought nothing of having my bones chopped out and metal ones put back in to replace them, they saved my life. However, now my metal bones are getting old and I have days where I just wanna chop it off.

# 8 NUTROPENIA IN ROOM 6

many people will know what neutropenia is. Well, I'll give you a little science lesson. Your blood is made up of many components, one of which is your called your neutrophils. This part of your blood is very important and is connected to your immune system. When these levels are on zero, you are susceptible to infection and have to be *very* careful. These levels had to be tested regularly when you were at home, if you ever got to go home that is. If your levels dropped, your chances of picking up an infection doubled. Socialising with friends and family became difficult in case someone had the snivels, as to me with no immune system the snivels could turn into a massive infection.

Even eating food kept on a hot plate was a big no no; it had to be all fresh or not at all. When you keep food hot on a hot plate, it produces little tiny microscopic bugs which would not affect the everyday person at all but when your levels are on zero those little bugs would run wild in my body. To know when or if you had an infection, you had to constantly take your temperature whilst your levels were low and if it creeped above 37.5 and headed toward 38 degrees, I had to contact the home care team to get me in my local hospital for antibiotics asap, just in case any infection decided to run riot in my body and attack my bionic leg, as apparently bugs love metal work!!

To no surprise, every chance I had to go home, my neutrophils dropped to zero and my temperature rocketed within a day, meaning that in the 16 visits I was able to go home in the year of 2000-2001, I spent every one of them in The Kent and Canterbury Hospital having antibiotics administered. *Oh the joys!*

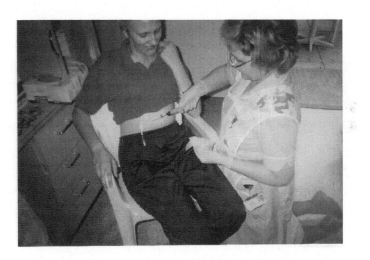

It is really important whilst on chemotherapy that if you get the chance to go home, your homecare team in the local area has to be on the ball, as they need to be able to visit once or even twice a day if needed.

I had a wonderful homecare team: they looked after me like I was part of their family. They were able to get strong drugs like morphine to me fast and rush blood tests to get results quickly. This meant that when I needed antibiotics, I could just turn up at the hospital and a room would be ready and waiting for us. The team would liaise with all my doctors and nurses so they knew everything that was happening and we were worry free. Believe it or not, we really were worry free in the knowledge that anything medical was covered. Don't get me wrong, I had cancer and my leg had a chunk of metal shoved in it, we had worries but we knew we could rely on them.

Away from cancer and the London hospitals, there were a lot of medical side effects that I suffered with. My main problem was that my blood levels didn't seem to want to pick themselves up after the chemo treatments. I ended up having to have a lot of other drugs to help my body work properly and recover ready for the next round of chemo. The worst drug was the GCSF….. "The Bee Sting". It was an injection that I had to have to boost my blood levels. I'm not sure exactly how it worked, but it has something to do with the bone marrow and helping the body produce more blood. All I know is that it was called "The Bee Sting" for a reason, OMG it was so painful and after the jab, your body would ache all day… Ouchy. It felt like I spent a lot of time in my local hospital and we really got to know the doctors and nurses. One man that made a very big impact on my treatment recovery was Geraint Lee. He was a SHO at the time, now I hear he's a big shot baby consultant and we are so proud.

Geraint was the one person my family and I were pleased to see when we arrived at our local hospital; he understood what I needed and how to talk to me, and that was important. Although I think he had the fright of his life the first time we met.... Picture this ...Room 6, pale blue walls, with children's cartoon images painted on each of them, a telly on the wall, my own private shower room, a patio with a table and chairs and not forgetting my mums very own pull out bed. Classy!!

I was slumped on a chair in my room with my pyjamas on, hugging a sick bucket with beads of sweat rolling down my bald head. I remember he knocked on the door and came in, taking one look at me he stepped back toward the door, he appeared a little taken back, but proceeded to say, "Are you ok??" followed by my "what do you think, there's sick everywhere!!!!" and from then we all hit it off.

Each visit to the hospital was made easier. Geraint and the nurses used to use room 6 as a stopping ground; they were super naughty, and they would come and hide from all the horrible tasks, whilst keeping me company of course.

I remember just after Christmas, Geraint brought their Christmas works do photos down to show me. It was fancy dress and they all looked bladdered, it was so funny. There was a feeling of being normal for just a short time, but those moments were really important. As a family, we couldn't thank him enough.

After a few months of visiting Room 6, I started to gather a bit of a reputation on the ward; all the doctors and nurses knew me and I certainly kept them busy with diva demands. I remember on one occasion when I became unwell at home in the stomach/bottom department *again*, my dad had called the on-call doctor and he wasn't sure what to do with me other than give me pain killers, which were making the problem a lot worse.

My dad had to call the homecare team, as even though it was late at night he felt it I was better off in hospital, so we got packed up and set off. The journey to the hospital was excruciating as my tummy/bottom was writhing. When I got there, they hooked my Hickman line up with a morphine pump, which I could administer myself by pressing the button every 5 mins, however after an hour I became very distressed and I was sure the pump was not working.

When I was in pain the only emotions I felt were stress and frustration, I never felt sad or scared, I just needed it to be over. A student nurse took a look at it and she tried the pump herself, and behold...... it had jammed, so the lovely young nurse decided to flush my line out as she felt the problem was my line and not the pump.... I disagreed, never the less she toddled off. Five minutes later, she arrived back in my room with a flushing kit.

I was in so much pain and my dad was starting to look worried so I just let the nurse do her thing, and apparently maths was not her strong point. She detached my line and before I could say anything, she very quickly pushed through 100 mls of saline fluid through. However, the pump consisted of the machine itself, a line of tube and that then attached to my Hickman line. The nurse had detached my line from the wrong end, leaving the tube attached and forgetting that it was full of morphine; funnily enough, the pain disappeared very quickly. I could not tell you how much morphine she pushed through my line or even how quick it was, all I knew was I felt very good and slightly sleepy and.... she got a telling off. That day was one to remember; although I can laugh now, I will never forget the pain I felt during that time and the worst part was that my leg felt fine. I didn't really have much bother with that, but the rest of my body was very messy.

The day after 'Morphine Gate' as we call it, they sent out a surgeon to take a look at me. They felt that I may need to have temporary colostomy bag as my digestive system was not performing very well. This surgeon walked around the hospital like he was god, every one bowed to him and I was told to be polite…..hmmmmm…. Can people really become a higher power?? I'm not sure: I was a fiery teenager, I knew what I wanted and no one was going to tell me what to do. I could hear him arrive by the desk and one of the nurses Linda asked him, "Would you like me to come in with you?" he replied by saying "No, there will be no need": famous last words… Bear in mind I was in a lot of pain and I had been sent through the roof with morphine the day before, so I was a little groggy.

He let himself in my room without knocking, which pissed me off 100%, walked over to me and started poking at me…. Bad move!…. I let rip at this man, there could have been some swearing and possibly telling him to bugger off a few times….. I could see the nurses outside the room giggling their heads off, and Linda felt it best to come in and offer him some support. Funnily enough, she persuaded him that it would be best to knock me out to take a better look at me as there was no way he was coming near me whilst I was awake. 'Bottom gate' was sorted rather promptly and this surgeon man decided it was best to just give me drugs instead of cutting me open. All I heard in my head was Yoda saying, *"Decision good, me thinks."*

On a serious note, I'm told I had a few close calls during my treatment. Although I don't remember them clearly, my family do. There were a few times where the pain was so bad that the drugs they gave me knocked me out for a few days. It is hard to hear your family say, "You scared me last night!" Thinking that they were preparing for me not to wake up is a hard thought to deal with.

I remember on one occasion when I became unwell whilst at home and when my dad rang the hospital, they explained there were no free beds and I would have to be diverted to another hospital for my antibiotics. This meant there was an hour and a half drive to another hospital and to top it off it was snowing. That night was the worst night I have ever had throughout my whole treatment. The hospital I ended up at had no idea what to do with me; they shoved me and my mum in a room which was cold and very uninviting. The ward I was on had no Hickman line trained nurses, so to get my antibiotics they had to page a doctor and he woke me up every time they were due. At my hospital, they just found my tubes and shoved it in, no waking me up or anything. I felt so poorly and to be honest I was a little scared that night. I'm not sure my mum slept at all, she was so worried, but when morning came we couldn't wait to find out if they had freed a bed up for me at my local hospital.

The nurses at Ashford were rubbish when it came to bed side manner, I couldn't believe how stroppy they were. When I asked for some breakfast they said they "only had toast left now, it's a bit cold but it'll do for you!" and when it came it was like eating cardboard with thick sticky butter! That was my cue to grab for the sick bucket! Luckily enough, by mid-morning my local hospital had arranged for me to be transferred back to them. Both my mum and I were really happy, however I wasn't looking forward to the journey there. I was in pain and I felt so rough, but I knew it was the best thing to do. So a car picked both me and my mum up and set off on an hour journey.

It had been snowing overnight and I was wrapped up in millions of layers; I had three jumpers, two scarfs, a woolly hat and some very thick gloves, as I didn't want to risk getting an infection from the cold. I remember the drive being very bumpy and not very comfortable. It felt like it took forever, but we got there in one piece and the driver went to get me a wheelchair.

He was ok up until that point, but when he sat me in the chair and put me on the pavement in the snow and proceeded to unpack our stuff and just left both me and my mum out on the pavement in the cold with all our stuff in hand (he didn't even help us into reception), my opinion of him reduced slightly. At one point, I wanted to swipe him with my crutches but my mum always tried to make the best of everything so she bundled our stuff in the foyer and came back for me as the driver just drove off in the icy weather, leaving us to it.

When I got into the foyer, I managed to get onto my crutches and get to the ward where they were ready and waiting for us. Linda got me wrapped up in bed and took over the whole situation. My mum was relieved that they could clean up my Hickman line properly and sort out my antibiotics. Linda gave me several cups of tea to try and warm me up and then I got some proper sleep. The next day Linda told me to "never do that again to her..." and that I "scared her yesterday" then proceeded to ask me if I wanted a bacon sandwich for breakfast, which I replied to her with "I'll try not to and yes please!", which was followed by a big hug.

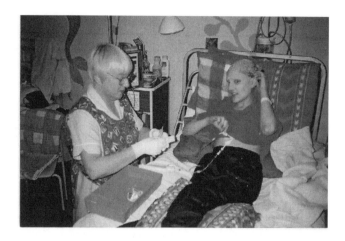

In that moment as I took a chunk out of my bacon sandwich, I worried for my family as if Linda had those thoughts then maybe they did. My mum and I communicated with an unspoken smile, which we used for all situations. She knew every one of mine, and I knew every one of hers. Believe it or not, I knew when my folks were sad and when they were scared: they were as easy to read as a book.

# 9 I'M DONE

The end was in sight and I could see my last cycle of chemo approaching. I was so excited, no more morning puking and maybe I could put a little bit of weight on... Yay....my heart was happy but my brain was a little scared, but as usual my body and I worked together to run to the finish line. During my last cycle of chemo, I pushed my physio and really made an effort when it came to my eating; I wanted a strong finish. On my last day, I knew it was the end but I just couldn't bring myself to want to leave; it was like leaving my family and I would never see them again. Not only that, I was seriously petrified. It had been roughly 10 months and my world had left me behind. It was time to see if reality would let me back in. My dad arrived at the hospital to pick me and my mum up. I hugged everyone, which took about an hour, and it was time to go home.

When chemo had totally finished, mentally I found it difficult being on my own for the first time in a whole year. It was like…. "here you go, there's your life back, do with it as you wish…" Well for a while there I got a little bit lost but I managed to regain some self-belief. Though it was hard, I feel like for me it was the best way to deal with it. I had just spent a whole year non-stop with my mum and dad, they never left my side, so it was quite a big adjustment being on my own. I'm sure most people could imagine the fear and turmoil I was going through in my mind, well times that by a million! I was so scared going out there into the world. I suppose my cancer and my hospital family felt like my security blanket, but I knew the only way I was going to get through it was to put a smile on my face every day and hold my head high, but this was it I was done with hospitals, drugs, blood tests and chemo. FREEDOM!!!!!

I so desperately wanted to go back to college to finish my Beauty and Holistic Therapy level 3 qualification, to really make something of myself, so the first thing I had to do was get off my crutches… for real this time, not cheat by tottering around on them. It was time to take a leap of faith and it was up to my physio Maggie to get me through it. She decided to put me to the middle of the room and take my crutches off me!!!! She said, "Ok walk to me!"… OMG NO WAY! Ouchy….

Maggie looked me in the eye and said, "You can do it, look at what you have achieved so far, a few little steps is nothing!" So, in my bright red fluffy socks, I slid my toes forward and tipped my weight onto my left leg and with a gasp in my breath I did it… kind of walking….. "Again….. again…", Maggie said in excitement, clapping her hand like she had won the lottery! We were both really excited and over the coming weeks I pushed as hard as possible. I only had a couple of months until the college year started again, so I needed to be steady on my feet. The day I binned my crutches was a great day.... I had beaten cancer and learnt to walk again all in the space of a year..... What next..... Well, it was time to make up for all my lost life experiences.

My time was spent saying yes to as much as possible, the need to fill the empty spaces in my life was immense. I had to rebuild my life from scratch, it wasn't like I only had a month off, I was out for a year and a half and all my friends had progressed in their lives. Part of me felt left behind as they were meeting partners and making life plans, however my friends were very supportive, and it actually gave me a chance to meet new people and make new friends.

# 10 MY ADVENTURES

When I was in hospital, I never really knew what the Teenage Cancer Trust was all about. It was not until my treatment was finished and my life was saved the TCT touched my heart and my appreciation for them was, and still is, massive. I have been finding it really difficult to actually put into words what the charity has done for me over the years and how I feel about it, although I do know that once you have encountered the TCT in your life they will always be there for you. Even though my treatment had finished, the TCT continued to be a big part in my life. I have many wonderful memories with the TCT and they continue to grow as the years go on. Even to this day, they are giving me and my family experiences we never thought possible. Everything I did was an adventure, I made sure that I took each experience and made the most of it.... I mean some of things I've done..... AMAZING!

Throughout the year, the charity holds many events to raise money and awareness for teenagers and young people suffering with cancer. One of the many events they hold is an excellent event called the 'Find Your Sense of Tumour' weekend. This was where patients and ex patients could get together and socialise with like-minded people, and most of all people who understand what they had been through. It's not like we've just had the flu; most of the teenagers have stared death in face and shown him the single finger salute with a polite gesture of 'come back later I'm busy'! It is important that we were treated normally and that is exactly what the TCT did. The event is not just open to TCT patients, but it is open to patients who were not getting the chance to experience a TCT unit and generally were treated in their local children's hospital.

The weekend consisted of talks from ex patients, talks from hospital/doctor experts, talks from members of the TCT and best of all a lot of fun. FYSOT is held at Centre Parks in Nottingham's Sherwood Forest. They put us up for the weekend and give the charity the use of the conference centre, which was our base whilst we were there. I have been to this event several times and each time I've been I have met loads of new and interesting people, some of which I still keep in contact with today. I was surprised at some of the stories told by patients and saddened by their experiences.

It is hard to believe that there are so many young people out there still being diagnosed late and treated poorly in hospital. These events were soooo important to me as not only do I love to talk, but I needed to talk to other people experiencing the same thoughts and feelings as I was. Maybe knowing I was not alone in the mental anguish of treatment, helped me figure my own head out.

## My most memorable FYSOT weekend

I don't know about yourselves, but I haven't kept in touch with many friends from school years. Most of that is to do with life moving in different directions and turning into adults.

However, there is one particular person who I feel I will always have a connection with at school, Joanne Sprawson. Though she is married now and is a Mrs. Brodie, she had breast cancer at 16 and was the youngest to be diagnosed in the UK at the time.

Joanne had all her treatment in our local hospital, which meant she had not come into contact with the TCT. I followed her treatment as much as possible on the news and in the papers, as she was so young apparently that was news! It is difficult to keep in contact with people when you are travelling to hospital, so Joanne and I kept in touch by good old fashion post.

When I got diagnosed at 17, I decided not tell too many people as I didn't really want too much fuss, and it also saved those awkward moments of, "How are you?" "What have you been up to?" and "Are you better now?" (lol someone people can be so dumb!) However, when treatment was over, Joanne and I got back in touch and I decided to invite her along to the Find Your Sense of Tumour weekend. I thought it would be a good opportunity for Joanne to ask questions and meet other teens who had cancer in their lives.

As Joanne was quite young when she had breast cancer, she didn't get to meet many other teens going through the same experiences. Thankfully, she embraced the experience of the weekend. I was so glad I took her to meet all my friends and to this day I have fab, fab memories of that weekend.

*Thank you Jo. X*

RAH craziness is amazing.

The biggest event for me in the TCT calendar was the week of concerts at the Royal Albert Hall.

The first few concerts I attended were as a patient; it was my chance to meet some other people who had finished their treatment and talk about how we felt. Mind you, I don't remember talking too much about treatment, more about music, TV and boys lol.

The day consisted of a little gathering of teenagers with Susie and Nigel, who are now part of the Education team within the TCT. We were based in a room high up in Royal Albert Hall near the top, where there were keyboards and musical instruments laid out for us to play with.

The day consisted of a lot of laughing and some very tone deaf music (*from what you've learnt about Susie so far I think you can create the image of craziness yourselves*)! Half way through the day we had some pizzas delivered for tea, which were very messy as we didn't really have plates or anything to eat off ..... like a table!

We had a great time though, and about an hour before the show was about to start, some people from the BBC news team arrived and somehow I ended up doing an interview with a reporter, which I was told by my dear friend Ross, was put on the national news pretty much live. He rang me the next day to ask if it was actually me.

The concerts themselves were amazing: I really enjoyed them. The first night we saw Marti Pellow and Emma Bunton, then on the second night we were seeing The Who. I have to say I wasn't really sure who they were but I was told they were old school rock so I knew I would love it.

Now a funny story always crops up every time The Who night gets mentioned in our house, as that day my blonde colours really shone through. During the day we had a little music workshop where we were all playing the instruments with a bloke called Roger. I was showing off my keyboard skills. It was great, we spent a good couple of hours having fun, making a drone of a noise which was supposed to be music, and before we knew it, it was time for pizza.

The whole day was great. I had taken my friend Tony and we had a blast, we were treated like super stars all day, we felt amazing. After tea, we went for a drink at the bar before the concert started, and when it was time to take our seats Roger said, "Right guys enjoy the show I'll see you later!" Of course I then said, "Are you not staying for the show!" He laughed and said "Caz......." Patted me on the back and walked off......

OMG I was completely oblivious until..... Boom, Boom, Boom.... the music started and our Roger who we had spent the day with comes swinging out on stage, microphone flying in the air and gave a little wave in our direction, with me screaming "OMG what's Roger doing on stage? Is he in the band?!!! WOW!" I think that is in one of my top ten embarrassing moments.....

Not counting the time I went running up to this chap who had super long curly black hair and was as tall as a giant saying " OMG will you sign my shirt? I know you are famous but I've forgot your name" he kindly signed it with a smile on his face... as I looked down to see .... Brian May!! I'm telling you, I give blondes a bad name!

I had a fantastic time at the concerts and couldn't wait for next year to come round. Susie and Nigel asked if I could help out next year with looking after the teenagers. I felt completely flattered and said YES in and instant. The TCT invited teenagers from all of the units in the UK, some teenagers who came on their own and were quite shy, and shy is not something I am aware of. I spent my time encouraging them to talk and enjoy their day and feel comfortable knowing they were not alone. The music workshops were loads of fun: this year they had been given a room which was a little more practical, there was more space and the toilets were closer! The patients had the chance to briefly learn a musical instrument during the day or do some song writing. Some of the songs they came up with were so funny, the most memorable was "Chocolate Monkeys"

Tom Gray was the fantastic conductor for the day; he would orchestrate the whole operation so it ran smoothly, he was great with the teens and each year he brought some little helpers from the London College of Music to teach the instruments. At the end of the workshop, the song was recorded so the patients could have a fun memory of the day to take home. When the music workshop was over and their fantastic music had been made, the patients got the opportunity to go back stage to enjoy a healthy posh meal from the restaurant where the celebs had their dinner. It was amazing to see some of their faces when a celeb walked in to get a cup of coffee, there were even a few occasions where the odd rockstar would pop in and sit down for dinner with the teenagers. I remember having dinner with Ronnie Wood and his son Jessie one year; *that was fun*. I am fully aware that he would probably not remember our dinner but we do and it was great! After we had all stuffed ourselves silly on the best cooked food I have ever had in my life, it was time for the concert and the teenagers were given their tickets and were free to disperse and have a wander round The Albert Hall until the doors opened...... to the bar!!!

The hustle and bustle of being back stage at the Royal Albert Hall was amazing, and I knew after that first year I would be helping out for as long as they would have me. I volunteered for this job for about 7 years after this, and for me it was about giving back, doing my part and really helping where I could. Each year was so different. I loved it, and with my pass I could go anywhere I wanted. Over the years there were other patients would come and help out with me. Bev, Kate and Kelly were the usual people that came along during the years. On occasion, we would help out the production team. I know we were only doing skivvy jobs but it was so much fun, we seemed to be able to get away with anything! When Goldie Looking Chain were performing as a support act, they were crazy good, they spent the whole music workshop with the patients before the show and one member of the band promised a patient she could have a sweat band for her bald head. So me and Bev went knocking on their dressing room door demanding they follow through and we came back with all sorts of goodies for her, *they were so nice.* My adrenalin was generally on a high for the whole week, every year when I came back the team were there with open arms and part of me knew it couldn't last forever but I didn't care, being treated like a normal person felt important. It took those seven years for me to rebuild my day to day life to the same level of importance and when I was ready I flew the nest. The guys from the charity presented me with a massive bunch of flowers, which I was not expecting, and long line of people waiting for a hug.

Obviously I met a few famous faces along the way. I don't like to namedrop but...!!

Marti Pellow, Emma Bunton, and Pete Townsend, Eric Clapton, Tom Jones and.....

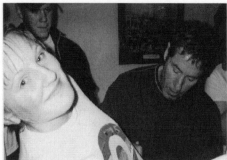

Rodger Daltrey

Michael Watson

Brian May

Chris Martin

Kelly Jones

Liam Gallagher

Paul Wellar

The Doves

Supergrass

Tim Fram

James Nesbit

Aswad

Suggs

Some more people from Madness...............

Nigel Kennedy                        Rodger Daltry

Simon Hanson

Bill Bailey

Samantha Bond

Steve Coogan

Simon Pegg

Matt Lucus

David Walliams

Jimmy Carr

Ricky Gervais

Rob Brydon

Noel Fielding

Jools Holland

Chris Drifford

Ruby Turner

Terry Walker

Dave Gilmour

Beverley Knight

Tom Jones

Ronnie Wood

Jessie Wood

Ricky Martin

Rodger Daltry

Some lads from the Artic Monkeys..........

Some more lads from the Artic Monkeys..........

Lemar

Tinie Tempah

Labrinth

Rizzle Kicks

Caroline Flack

Des Murphy

Through The Teenage Cancer Trust, I have been on so many adventures and experienced many new things. I can safely say that I would never have had the opportunity to experience any of these things without the Teenage Cancer Trust and I hope that they continue to do what they do best for many of their patients throughout the UK.

## Turks and Caicos

My adventures continued outside of the TCT, and I continued to take every opportunity offered to me...... I would be silly not to!

Whilst in hospital you are visited by many people, one of which is like a social worker, I wasn't sure if that was her real job title but something like that.

Her job was to help you with applying for benefits, travel arrangements and really anything she could help you with. Being in hospital was expensive and my folks did their best to keep a roof over our heads. There were times I knew they were struggling but they never said anything. Having two hospitals meant I had two social worker ladies, which meant our support was covered from all angles. On a rare occasion, they would be able to provide you with fun free things like trips out and nights in hotels which was cooooool, but there was one occasion when I had a letter through the post at home informing me that I had been nominated by both of my social worker ladies for a place on the Free Spirit Trip.

At the time, I had no idea what this was, so my dad and I did some investigating and found out that The Free Spirit was a charity which takes patients who are off treatment to the Turks and Caicos Islands in the Caribbean! OMG I could not believe that I had been picked by both of my hospitals to go on this trip of a lifetime, I was buzzing! Obviously I felt the need to make a few phone calls to ensure that it wasn't some sort of prank…. And after putting the phone down my excitement level went through the roof.

The letter required me to send a form back with all my details and confirmation that I was interested in going, OMG who wouldn't want to spent 17 nights in the Caribbean parent free, with a bunch of strangers for the trip of a lifetime???? As my treatment had only just finished when I got the letter it was something really *cool* to look forward to whilst I was recovering, it gave me the determination to get back on my feet and off my crutches as soon as I could.

During the following weeks, I received a letter inviting me to a team building weekend, which gave me an opportunity to meet my fellow travelers. They came from all over the UK so it was very exciting, there were to be six boys and six girls all roughly the same age. When I finally got off my crutches, I could not wait. The weekend couldn't come fast enough.

I had packed my bag a good week before I went so I was ready, and when the day came my folks drove me to Green Park. This trip was to be an adventure, not just a holiday, but a chance to be free from cancer and find out who I really was. Meeting my new travelers for the first time was a little nerve racking but I just jumped in with two feet and got the party started. It wasn't long before everyone had sent their folks home as it was obviously so uncool to have them hanging about. The weekend gave us the opportunity to bond and get all our "where did you have your cancer questions?" out of the way, so that when it was time to meet at the airport we would just be excited about our destination. I got on with everyone, however, Jess and I got on like a house on fire: we were like two peas in a pod, and I just knew we'd have a great time together.

Sadly though, when it was time to meet at the airport, the one person I had make the best connection with wasn't there. I was told that during the three weeks we were apart, Jess had taken ill again and wouldn't be able to join us in the Turks and Caicos Islands, and although I knew before we got to the airport, I was still sad. In Jess's absence another young lady called Lorraine was invited in her place and we all did our best to make her welcome and feel like part of the group. I was full of adrenalin and ready to start my adventure and as we got on the plane, a sense of freedom came over me.

OMG EPIC!

It was the most beautiful setting ever, with a horizon which went on forever, sun set cruises, treasure hunting on a deserted Island, swimming in crystal clear waters with a friendly wild dolphin...... bonfires with peaceful evenings just watching the sun go down, Halloween partying in crazy fancy dress, driving golf buggies on a five star golf course with pink flamingos just flying around, having a BBQ on Gecko Island with lizards all over the place, tropical fruit being picked from the tree and then put on our plates.....amazingly juicy.

We slept a lot, we drank our weight in water every day and used more sun cream than I have ever imagined, I ran out on day 6! My memories and feelings from this trip are amazing, it felt like I found myself and reminded myself why I had spent the last year fighting like a gladiator to live and embrace every second of every day. I realised why life is so important.

Some people say they love the smell of freshly cut grass, but not many people stop and take the time to enjoy it, well this trip reminded me of all the things I didn't want to miss out on. I could have stayed forever but I knew my life had purpose now and I was ready to go and live again!!!

This trip had a profound effect on me. I found peace and freedom within myself which I never thought I would ever get back. I know that was the point, I just didn't get it before then.

I made a few lifelong friends on this trip, some of which I'm still in contact with today, *"Hey Big T"* and sadly some of which relapsed shortly after we arrived back home and lost their battle with cancer. *Always in my memories.*

Back in England, I received a letter from Jess's mum. It had a letter from Jess telling me how sorry she was she couldn't make the trip and hoped I had good time. She told me to stay in touch, however her mum sent this to me because Jess lost her battle with cancer and felt she would have liked me to have it.  Although I was sad, I knew that she had really been suffering so I found peace knowing that.

*R.I.P Daniella, Katie, Jenny and Jess, love you girls, be free!*

## NYC

When my legs were up and running properly there was no stopping, life started to become fun again and it was like one adventure after the other......

I feel I should mention my little trip to New York as it was another one of those spontaneous moments. Myself and Kelly Scott were asked as patients by the TCT to be on a judging panel for FiFi Awards in London. Again my knowledge of the world was limited and I had to research it, and it turns out it was the Fragrance industry awards which are a pretty big deal. Being on a judging panel is a huge honour. I had to make sure that they knew what they were letting themselves into, but apparently the FiFi awards were sponsoring the TCT.... Awesome!

My role was to judge the aroma of the fragrance and place them in order of best to worst and if I can remember correctly Kelly's was to do with packaging. When I turned up to a fancy hotel in London, of which I can't remember the name, there were a couple of rather posh people there to help with the judging process, which was a relief as they all smelt the same to me! I can't remember their names exactly but I can remember their..... how do you say...... Poshness (*I'm not sure that's a real word but I'm using it!*) There was a magazine editor, a diamond jeweller, a chap in fashion and one other upper class crazy lady, how could we get it wrong between us???

The day was very heavy, my head was spinning, the smell was intense but we had fun, and to end the day we were treated to lunch in a very posh afternoon tea restaurant, there were so many knives and forks just for a sandwich lol. When it was time to go home, we all had the opportunity to choose a perfume set to take home with us. I took the J Lo set; it had the perfume, body lotion and a body wash..... Very nice.  It didn't end there though.

Kelly and I were to accompany Simon Davis, chairman of the TCT, to the Dorchester Hotel for the actual FiFi awards evening. We felt like royalty, it was amazing and I think Simon enjoyed having a lady on each arm!  When we arrived at our table, we found Dr Adrian Whiteson OBE, the honorary president of the Charity, together with his wife, Myrna Whiteson MBE who is the driving force in developing Teenage Cancer Trust's International Conferences on Cancer and the Adolescent.

OMG I had to mind my P's and Q's! The evening was amazing, the awards ceremony ran smoothly and when the awards that we judged came up, our photos came up on the big screen and we were both presented with a bunch of flowers, it was soooo cool.  As the evening went on, we had a *very posh* dinner and just enjoyed the music and conversation.  It was sad when it came to the end but we loved every minute and couldn't thank the TCT anymore if we tried, but it was time to get back to normal again, until.......

Two weeks later I received a phone from Simon and he told me that the lady who won first prize in raffle that night couldn't go and wondered if we wanted her tickets.... Hmmmmmm, what raffle and what tickets? Oh just two flight tickets and two tickets front and center at the FiFi Awards in New York City!!!! OMG Obviously I said yes and hung up very quickly to ring Kelly, and when I knew she was up for it, my excitement level just rocketed once again, we were off to NYC.  Now they say the best trips are the ones you don't plan as it allows a little freedom. Well, we didn't have much time to plan... we had just about enough time to book a hotel, pack our bags and get to the airport, ok that may be a little bit of an exaggeration but we were short of time lol. Before we knew it, Kelly and I were on a plane and my adventurous side came back to play.

The plane ride was fine, no crashing, and by the time we got the hotel we were shattered as we were on Greenwich mean time (GMT).  Kelly suggested that we should stay up as long as possible so we could readjust our body clocks..... she's a clever girl!  The trip wasn't a long one, we only had a 5 days to fit everything in, and our time was a little short if we wanted to visit all the sights.  We both had a few places we wanted to see, so Kelly sorted our plan of action out and we went everywhere! I have some cool pictures of places I only ever dreamt of going.... uptown, downtown, The Bronx, Statue of Liberty, Soho, Chinatown and the subway.

As there was a reason for our visit to NYC, we had to fit the FiFi awards in our busy schedule... Oh so difficult! On the night of the awards, we got all glammed from head to toe. I was in my pink ball gown and Kelly had a slinky black number on: we were ready for the red carpet. The awards in NYC were a lot bigger and as Kelly and I hit the red carpet we got papped from all angles, mind you they had no idea who we were but we loved it! *Strike a pose!*

We both learnt a great deal of independence during our time together and I knew when I came home it would be time for me to really think hard about my future and make some decisions. I couldn't live at home with my folks forever and I knew it was time for me to be out in the world, find love and be really happy. This trip really did that for me, I had such a great time with Kelly we talked and laughed a lot, I even remember having a few D & M (deep and meaningful) conversations which were good. On our arrival home, it was once again time to get back to reality.

# 11 MR SMITH

Let me take you back a little.....

At 19, I'd never been in love before and life after cancer was hard. I felt as though I would be on my own forever, living with my parents and leading the most boring life ever.

During a RAH concert, I was volunteering as a helper and I met a group of patients from Sheffield. Within this group there were approximately 5 patients and 3 nurses, and as usual I put my foot in it and mistook an ex-patient for a nurse, he was a little older than the other patients that usually came along. This broke the ice and got a conversation going with a good naming introduction, "Hi my name's Caroline... What's yours?" He replied by saying, "My name's Neil and this is my mate Tim". It was actually nice to talk to someone of my age group about the adult side of treatment, and no I don't mean the naughty side, I just mean thoughts of living away from your parents for example. As the day developed, I thought I noticed a little flirting going on. It had been a long time since this had happened to me and I didn't want to misread the signs so I accepted the olive branch of friendship and Neil and I exchanged phone numbers. From that day, we texted each other every day. The messages started with 'mate' and 'chick' then slowly the messages turned into 'babe' and that was it. Mr. Smith and I were becoming smitten.

A month passed from the day of the concert and Neil and I were in contact a couple of times each day either by text or phone; we were really getting on well. During one of our many phone conversations, we planned to meet at the Teenage Cancer Trust Bandana launch in Leister Square (London). This was in 2003. Well I took this opportunity with both hands and went for it. My plan was that evening to knock his socks off, and knock them off I did. After a few tipples of good old vodka and cranberry juice, I went in for the kill, and as we kissed the room completely disappeared and fireworks filled my tummy. I can safely say from that night we were a couple. I just knew that I really liked him and I wanted to get to know him a little better.

That evening I stayed with my good friend Big T in London and planned to travel home on the train the next day. When we woke in the morning, I was floating on cloud 9. I was so happy, I turned my phone on super quick to see if he had texted me…. It said, "Good morning gorgeous, call me when you're up, I'm on the train xxx." And that was it, my heart was fluttering once again, something was happening and it made me feel so happy. I hadn't smiled that much in a really long time. When Big T put me on the train home, I was able to call Neil. I was so nervous, thoughts running through my head, "does he like me?" and "will he want to travel to me?" At the time, Neil lived in Derbyshire and I lived in Kent. "Was this possible, can long distance really work?" We talked for a while, none of it really made any sense. We just kind of mumbled to each other, though it was clear that he couldn't wait to see me again. We arranged to talk properly when we got home which felt like it took forever. I just wanted to snap my fingers and be there straight away.

As we were both ex-patients, I felt as though I didn't have to explain myself to him, I was so happy.

We were a couple and our lives got crazy; we blissfully travelled back and forth for months enjoying every moment together and falling deeper and deeper in love than I had ever been before. It almost felt like a dream, the only sad thing is, that dreams aren't real and life is never that easy. One day I had just got back from college and the phone rang, which was a little unexpected as it was 4ish in the afternoon.

However, it was my beloved and was a nice surprise.... until.... I could hear him crying on the phone and I knew straight away what he was going to say, "babe, my cancer is back!!" We talked for a few minutes and he explained that he was going to be treated with radiotherapy and it was due to start the next day as he was a relapse patient. When I put the phone down, my heart raced and I crumbled. My dad phoned my mum to get her to come home asap. I then packed a very big bag as I had a feeling I was going to need it. I talked it all through with my parents and I remember my mum asking me if I loved him. I said "yes", and she knew that I was going that night to be with him and nothing was going to stop me.

I thought having cancer was hard, but watching someone you love go through treatment is harder. I knew how much pain Neil was in as I had been there and I understood how the medication worked. I believe that this connection helped both Neil and I as he didn't need to tell me when he was tired or in pain as I knew by the look on his face.

Over the next coming months, things started to move very quickly and our lives just turned into a haze. I helped look after Neil and his parents, whilst Neil had radiotherapy every day, and stayed whilst he had surgery to put a support rod in his leg to stabilise the diseased area. Neil's parents can't drive so they needed me to stay as long as I could, but I wanted to be there so they really didn't need to ask.

I hadn't really appreciated what my parents had been through until I found myself in a very similar situation. I stayed with Neil and his family for some time. The days turned into weeks and the weeks merged into many months. Before I knew it, about 6-8 months had passed and it was difficult. I found myself feeling very lost and insecure, though when we needed to we all pulled together. We made a very efficient team.

Neil recovered from his first relapse quite well and seemed to get back to his normal crazy self and so in January 2005 we decided to embark on a new adventure and move in together in Derbyshire. My mum and dad were sad to see me go, but they knew they would still be a very big part in my life and I knew they would always be there for me when I needed them. I couldn't believe it when we woke up together for the first time, we could walk around naked if we wanted, it was great. Unfortunately we didn't spend long in this particular house. We had to move shortly after... it was a renting thing. However, when we were finally settled in our second new house our lives started to pick up and we regained some normality. We finally had a proper grown up relationship and could make all our own decisions.

When I would think about our life, I didn't really make long term plans. I think that was just habit, the whole not knowing if you were going to live or die tends to make it difficult to plan for a future. We decided we would just plan for the here and now so it was.... fun, fun, fun and more fun on the agenda. However, life doesn't always go the way you plan and obstacles are generally thrown in to see if we're still awake. Mid 2005, Neil relapsed again. My heart sank for the second time and my mind wandered to a very bad place. I wasn't sure if I could do this again.

His treatment involved chemotherapy, and to me this meant sickness and balding. Neil was always surprising me, he seemed go through it with a full head of hair, very little sickness and a very strong determination. All I felt was true relief when he had finished. However, after this treatment he became very weak and if I had to be honest I wasn't sure how many times Neil could do this. In my mind I thought, 'well is this going to be our life now'. Cancer is difficult to understand and I wasn't sure that his cancer would ever really go. I wanted to believe it, but really deep down I was sad. I knew it wasn't good, I just didn't know how bad it was.

During one of our heart to heart conversations, for the first time Neil and I talked about future plans and life in general. He became very sad, as he always found it difficult to completely express himself and I was sure he never told me exactly how he felt. He kept a lot in, as he didn't want to burden me, which I can understand. At times I felt that Neil had forgotten that I had experienced cancer and how it made you think and feel. I know that sounds selfish, but I couldn't help it. However, I could imagine how it felt thinking that you may not be here to experience any of the life you planned and it scared me shitless.

During Neil's second relapse, he became very down and mid-way through his treatment he got progressively worse. It became difficult to communicate with him. He wouldn't let me into his emotions and I felt very isolated. I know it could sound a little selfish, but I felt like I needed more from him. I began to feel a little sad myself, as at times it was like I was a taxi driver back and forth from the hospital, a nurse when at home getting the pills ready and sorting out appointments and the bread winner going to work as much as I could. During this time we were living in a bubble, it was like we were watching ourselves on tele. It felt like this could never be happening, but it was. When his treatment ended, he had a scan to see if the chemotherapy had worked, and as far as the doctors could tell the cancer had disappeared for now. There was a sense of relief, though his mood was still very low. I found it difficult to understand at times as his treatment had finished, I thought his mood would pick up but it didn't.

I felt it was time he talked to someone professional, just to see if he could work out what was going on in his head. For a while there I didn't think he would do it, but he agreed and it turned out his sessions worked really well for him and he started to understand why he felt like he did and encouraged him to direct his feelings into poetry. Neil started writing some really deep and meaningful poems, it was his way of expressing himself to me, his folks and his friends. A couple of months passed and Neil was on the way to writing some amazing poems, it felt like we were gaining some normality back and life started to get better again, our moods had lifted and Neil and I were communicating like never before. Neil was the kinda guy that would hide his fears to the outside world.


Whenever we bumped into someone we knew, he would put on this, "Yeah we're all good!" attitude, but I could see into his eyes, I saw his pain and how he really felt. As his partner, all I could do was be there for him, his sessions seemed to go really well and his outlook on life was changing slightly. Don't get me wrong, he had some crazy demons in there fighting to take over his brain, but he was strong and I knew he could battle them.

When things started to look up, I would always wait for bad news, and unfortunately life took another evil turn for us. Neil started getting a pain near his hip joint and straight away we feared the worst. I wasn't sure how many times Neil could do this, my mind was in a place I don't want to go back to, and I could see him crumbling again.

My emotions were all over the place: I had a job as a holistic therapist, a partner who was extremely ill and a lot of people relying on me to fix everything.  We soon found out his cancer had continued to grow and this time it was affecting the lymph nodes in his legs. It caused so many complications and his care was about to become a full time job which I had to fit in around being a taxi driver, nurse and bread winner.  After we had received the confirmation that his cancer was back, Neil broke down to his lowest point, and for me I felt there was no other option than to create hope in all our lives.

I loved Neil so much and it hurt me every day when he was in pain, so I made a big decision. I felt as though it was right and I felt that for me I wanted to do it. Lying on our bed whilst cradling Neil as he sobbed in my arms I said, "Let's get married!!" He was in complete shock and laughed at me saying, "Are you serious??" "Yes!" I replied and I followed it with "the sooner the better!" It was mid-July and we would have loved to try and get married before the year was out, as I feared he wouldn't make it. However, there would be a lot to arrange and we had to get all our dates to match. Neil was so happy and excited, and it had been a long time since we had all seen this side to him. He was able to focus on something other than having cancer. Over the next couple of months, Neil continued with his treatment at the same time as making plans for our wedding. I feel that this new-found hope gave Neil a reason for living again. There were many occasions that I felt as though he was ready to give up, but I wouldn't let him. Looking back, I had only just found this man who was the light in my life and selfishly I wasn't about to let him go anywhere. I so desperately wanted to be his wife some day and I know if the cancer wasn't in the equation we may have waited a little longer, but I was so glad we didn't. It was perfect, I got to marry Mr. Smith.

When Neil had finished his current lot of treatment, he got an all clear scan from the doctor, meaning at that moment in time he was free from cancer, and it was time to plan our amazing wedding. The first thing he said to me was, "babe you have whatever you want". I responded with, "no it's a joint thing, we'll both decide," however secretly I knew I was having all I wanted (that was every bride's right surely he he he he).

The first thing we did was decide on the date and no matter what we would have to find companies that could fit us in for everything else. Yes, I was aware that this was slightly unconventional, but we didn't care, that was us. 21st January 2006 was to be our wedding day, all we had to do was book the church and we were cooking on gas. Now most people who know me would know that I am very organised and generally have a plan or list be it in mind or on paper, and this was to be no exception. I have had to be organised with hospital visits and sorting out medication so this would be a breeze..... surely? I set about writing a list of thing to book, order and buy. I had no idea how long these would be, however, all I could think of was Neil and how I could make him happy. Even though it was both of our days, I had a niggling feeling this would be the only chance we had. So when I had finished my lists, I sat back and took a good look.

My first thought was... we don't need white doves and mystical ring baring unicorns.. all we needed was each other and our friends and family, so I ripped up my first list and started again, but this time it was simple..... nice and simple. As we headed into Christmas 2005 with all the wedding plans nearly finished, Neil's health was difficult. Although the cancer was not there, he had been left with lethargy, anxiety and pain throughout his whole body.

Once Christmas was over, we were able to really concentrate on the finer details of the wedding, like favours and all the little stuff!! We had so much fun, there were smiles, laughing and plenty of love, and as our day got closer and closer the nerves set in. I can honestly say that all

I thought about was enjoying the day and making sure Neil was as happy and as healthy as could be.

I'll try not to bore with too much detail about our beautiful wedding but....... I arrived on time to a fully packed Heath Church in Chesterfield with a racing heart and sweaty palms, my tiara and dress were sparkling in the January sun and I felt like a princess. The service itself is a little bit of a blur; I remember singing some songs and trying to get the words right when it was my turn to say "I do".

All my planning meant that Neil got his 2 hour kip in the afternoon with not one of the guests being any the wiser and he didn't miss a thing. The meal was amazing: it looked good and tasted good, and I even had to get my mum to loosen my dress a little so that I could eat everything on my plate. We saved the big speeches for the evening as we only invited 20 people to the meal, but my dad said a few kind words, which were nice. Most of the evening guests understood why we split the day, which make it easier on our consciences.

When we arrived at the evening venue, our jaws just dropped, our little fairy helpers had done such a lovely job and the whole place looked like a red wine and gold gazebo. As the guests arrived, they were greeted by my dad and I. Neil couldn't stand for long periods of time so it was team Coleman to the rescue: my dad helped me with the meet and great, although believe me when I say that I had no idea who some of the people were as Neil's family is soo big.

We just smiled graciously and handed them some sparkling wine. As the evening progressed, it was time for speeches. Truly, I cannot remember the order everyone spoke in. My dad presented a lovely piece which was heartfelt, Neil's best friend Tim gave the cheeky and lovely best man speech, followed by Gaz who surprised everyone with his charming words as he would normally go for the laugh. My dear friend Susie also said a few words, which were beautiful, and finally to finish off the lovely Mr. Smith, my new husband and partner in crime, who said some really precious words for everyone to take with them in their hearts.

I didn't feel the need to say anything as I think they all pretty much covered how great we were! I'm sure that all the people that came to the wedding feel the same way I do about the day and the memories of the day will be in my heart forever. Best of all, our friends and family shared our special day with us.

The Teenage Cancer Trust came up trumps and arranged for the both of us to spend the week at Bovey Castle for our honeymoon, with full privileges to all activities, spa and restaurant. We didn't spend a penny! The owner at the time was Peter De Savary and he even sent a massive car to chauffer drive us there and take us home. 5 star class. We had a wonderful time: we used all the facilities, from facials to mini golf, from green laning to afternoon tea, and all the staff treated us like royalty.

Neil really enjoyed the spa treatments, which was funny as he was really uncertain before we went in but he had his facial and came running out saying.. "We have to have everything!" And that was it, he booked us in for as much as possible. We could not thank them enough.

When all the wedding excitement had calmed down, Neil and I tried so dearly to be a normal couple, but as the torment of summer rolled round our anxiety increased, his ugly friend pain reared its head, and Neil began to feel discomfort in his hip area again and I knew... I just knew in my heart that this time was not going to be easy.

When we went to see the consultant, he seemed quiet and not really saying much, which wasn't like him. However, he started by saying, "I'm so sorry". I am sure that's not a good thing when your doctor starts by saying sorry first. Neil being the strong and independent person he was, just replied, "So what's the plan". Neil had a lot to fight for now and he was determined to win this battle. Luckily enough, his consultant was a little bit of a rebel and tried Neil on some drugs that were not specifically for his cancer but there had been some positive research in its use. So that was it, a new drug and another summer of chemotherapy.

I refused to let bad thoughts swamp my mind this time; we were happy in love and married. Neil had enough to deal with and as a team both Neil and I were strong, but without his mum and dad (Anne and Harry) life would have been super difficult. Whilst I went to work at the salon, Anne and Harry would come down to our house and sit with Neil all day, making sure he ate in the afternoon and took the right tablets which I left out for him.

As the cancer grew, Neil's legs became more swollen and the lymphatic flow from his legs to his body seemed to be slowing down, which really started to restrict his movement. This made walking and general day-to-day tasks very difficult. Every morning and evening, I would do lymphatic massage to ease the swelling in Neil's legs, alongside the mammoth amount of pain relief he was taking.... Methadone, Morphine, Diamorphine, Oxycodone, Diclofenac, Naproxen, Ibuprofen and feeble Paracetamol, to name but a few. These drugs all had a purpose and were not to be taken all at once. At one stage, I felt like a pharmacist. I had to control not just Neil's pain relief but all his drugs, from things to make his tummy move, to things for lifting his spirit, and it was difficult. However, I am very organised, so during the evenings I would methodically get Neil's drugs ready in pots labeled with the times they were to be taken the next day.

Every day was a battle with the drug box and I could not be there 24/7, so I relied on Anne and Harry, but most of all I trusted Neil to only take what was in each pot. I know there were days when he would sneak some more pain relief as he couldn't cope and that was ok. I totally understood: to see the pain on his face was almost terrifying. I have felt pain in my life but every inch of him was writhing in agony pretty much all day and all night, and unfortunately Neil was starting to spend more time drowsy than awake.

Cancer is painful and I do not blame Neil for sneaking a few extra pills, but there were several occasions where he just took too many, though not on purpose. Neil honestly could not remember what and when he took them, and on two occasions I had to take him into hospital to have reversal drugs. This process is very painful for the recipient, as it does not just reverse the extra few tablets, it reverses all the drugs he had taken. Watching him go through this process was really hard. As he screamed out in pain, all I could do was cry. Looking back now, I really don't know what I could have done differently. Neil's head was in a place so far away that no one could help him; he just wrote more poems and tried to put on a brave face.

As Neil's chemotherapy came to an end, we had spent a lot of time in hospital. It pretty much felt like we were living there from time to time. The nurses were really accommodating toward myself, and Anne or Harry stayed with Neil as much as possible, as by this stage the smallest tasks like brushing your teeth, eating or having a wash became near impossible for him. For a while, I tried to believe that his symptoms were getting worse due to the chemotherapy, but I knew that something wasn't right.

Neil's consultant came to visit us up on the unit with results, however, again his facial expression wasn't reading very well. The previous day, Neil had gone for scan to see how the chemotherapy was working and his news wasn't good.

The doctor explained that the treatment had not worked at all and his tumours had continued to grow.

When he said 'tumours' my ears pricked up as I was thinking, 'how many does he actually have inside him'? We were never really told the extent of the tumours, all we really wanted to know was what treatment was next...... and that was it... that was the moment we were all dreading, his reply was, "we've run out of options for now, but we'll wait to see if something comes up!" Wait and see if something comes up.... OMG I wanted to smack him round the chops!! I didn't want to show how sad I was, so I stayed strong for Neil and his parents, but my insides were screaming as my heart broke into a million pieces and my world was officially dying.

Neil kept telling me that he'd never give up, but in the back of my mind, I began to prepare myself for the worst. Neil told me that we had to just be normal and not make a fuss, and subsequently he sent me to work. I didn't want to go to work as my head was all over the place, my heart was broken and work was the last thing on my mind, but I knew he was just trying to distract me and he was probably right.

Between me, Anne and Harry we took it in turns to stay at the hospital with Neil that week. The doctors didn't really want him to go home as day by day he began to deteriorate. I hated not being at the hospital, as it felt like I was missing precious time, but Neil wouldn't have it. He wanted me at work and after a hard week at the salon, it was my turn to stay at the hospital for the weekend. I was really looking forward to it.

On Friday 27th October 3pm, I was sat in a staff meeting at work, not really listening but thinking about Neil, when the work phone rang. Normally we ignored the phone during meetings but Cat was sat right next to it so she picked it up. It was Joy from the hospital. She was the nurse looking after Neil and she asked me if I was going to visit that evening?

My plan was to go up Saturday morning, but she said that Neil wanted to see me, so I said, "I'll pop up after work", which wasn't long, and then we got back to the meeting. After about five minutes, something came over me. I stood up, grabbed my bag and said, "I've gotta go." My boss just said, "yeah that's ok, ring me later and keep me posted." I didn't really know why I was leaving, I just had this weird feeling.

I jumped in the car and drove to the hospital, and the next thing I knew I had arrived. Sarah, one of the nurses, greeted me with a hug. She didn't beat around the bush, she just came out with it and said, "Are you staying tonight?" Hmmm...well I wasn't going to. She said, "You should, Neil's had a bad day and we're not really sure if he's going to make it through the night."

OMG those words were a little unexpected. The panic inside of me was erupting like a volcano, but I just couldn't express it to anyone as I needed to stay strong. Anne and Harry were already at the hospital, so I went straight to them to see how they were. It was stupid thing to think they were ok, as I already knew they would be in pieces, but Anne was in slight panic mode as if she was going to stay the night she needed to get her medication from home. So being the organiser and pillar of strength, I made a plan of action.

I popped in to see Neil just to give him a big hug and kiss and told him I love him and not to go anywhere, then I took Anne home leaving Harry at the hospital. We got Anne's medication and a change of clothes for us all and headed back to the hospital. In total, it was an hour and a half round trip, but it felt like forever.

When we got back to the hospital, I finally had the chance to sit down and be with my Neil. I knew he wasn't good, don't get me wrong I had hope in my heart, but he was really spaced out and beginning to not make much sense. Seeing him like that is one of the bad memories, he was in so much pain and I was helpless.

That night I felt as though I should contact Neil's friends Tim and Gaz, as I don't think I would have been able to forgive myself if I didn't give them a chance to see him, just in case. As far as phone calls go that was hard. I rang Tim and without actually saying, "get here now", I tried to hint on the urgency that he pop to the hospital that night. He was going to come in the morning, but I pushed the urgency in hope he understood. He agreed, and maybe I should have told him the truth, but I couldn't bring myself to say that Neil may die tonight so come and visit. I also asked him if he could ring Gaz, as I just couldn't make that phone call again. On the inside, I was like jelly and I knew I had to keep it together but it was hard.

When the boys finally arrived, Neil was not really with it, but I knew that he recognised them. They sat with him for hours and talked about old times from school and growing up.

Neil had a slight smirk on his face as if he was trying to express himself. I was glad I called them. It got late and both Tim and Gaz had to leave for the night. I made sure they were coming back the next day, as I knew Neil really needed them there. They probably had the same night as us; we didn't sleep well. That night was one of the hardest things I've ever had to cope with. As I watched him sleep, I made sure his chest moved up and down with every breath, praying that he would make it through the night.

When morning came, I went to check on Anne and Harry. They had been trying to get some sleep in the parents' room, and like me they didn't get much either. We all sat and watched Neil as he laid fighting for every breath. I was so proud of him, he promised me he would never give up and every breath he took he fought like the man I knew he was. My parents arrived to support us all along with Tim and Gaz. The day was like something out of the movies. I felt as though I was having an out of body experience, looking down on the world.

Mid-afternoon, Neil really started struggling to catch his breath, I informed Joy and she got Anne and Harry, who had gone for a cuppa tea, to come and sit with us all. That moment Neil looked peaceful; he had everyone he loved so dearly right next to him: his mum and dad, me, my folks and his best friends. I just knew the time was coming, so I held his hand. It felt like we were sat for ages.

I was watching a pulse beating in his neck, and my heart was beating in time. With a blink of an eye, it just stopped. I looked at his lips and they turned grey, his life just drifted away. I turned my head to look and Tim sat next to me and he knew. I remember him just saying, "Caz" and tears rolled down my face. Anne hadn't realised as she had her head down praying for hope, but her son had passed away.

From that moment, the raw emotion was so heavy you could feel it. I couldn't believe he was gone, just like that his heart stopped beating and the world decided it was his time. How is that fair...... ? Who really gets to decide our fate??? Why was it his turn and not mine??? If I could have swapped places right there and take away all the pain I would have. We were all in a daze, there were a lot of hugs and a lot of tears, and I cannot really remember much else from that day. I just didn't want to believe it was happening.

I had to go home to an empty house. Neil had gone, life as I knew it had gone, my world, my perfect.... all of it had gone. As you could imagine, the days that followed were crazy. We organised his funeral and my head and heart were in a place of emptiness. "What was happening?" "My husband had died.... Eh?" "What was I going to do?" Life as I knew it had gone again and my world was lost.

I know it sounds fast, well that's because it was, but when it came to the details of the funeral I let Anne and Harry decide what they felt Neil wanted. All I knew was that Neil did not want anyone wearing black to his Life Celebration.

It was all a little surreal: who plans their husband's funeral at 23 after only being married for 9 months and 1 week, picking what coffin I think he would have liked and what flowers he would have wanted on it... OMG that was too much.  And if that was not hard enough, when the funeral day came I was in auto pilot trying not to cry. As we walked in the church behind Neil, I looked around at all the people who came to see him off and the church was heaving. There were people standing wherever they could get a spot.

From the back to the front of the church it was packed, all with people who loved Neil.  During the service, I was completely out of it. When it was my turn to say something, I couldn't really see anyone, it was all a bit blurry. However, I read my bit I had written about Neil and how special he was and that we must all take something from his life and be inspired by his strength.

I felt like I was floating: all my senses were gone, I couldn't feel anything. For the rest of the service, I sat with mum and tried to put on a brave face. I even tried to sing the hymns, which Anne had chosen.  My mum held my hand and kept me together.

Before I knew it, the service had finished and people were starting to set off for the wake, and a surprise turned up in the form of the Chesterfield football team. They came to pay their respects; Neil was an avid Chesterfield fan and he went to most of the games.  Both the manager Roy McFarland and the coach Lee Richardson got off the bus and headed toward us... followed by the team. Lee put his arm around me and asked if it was ok to visit Neil's grave, as they had bought a football of flowers to place down. The players all threw some dirt into his grave in respect, Lee said a few words for inspiration and they headed back to the bus. Roy took Anne and looked after her. For me that moment was special. Without knowing it that team had given Neil a reason for living and to be able to thank them was a blessing.

"I told you the day was surreal."

When we got to the wake, I tried my hardest to talk to everyone but I just ended up walking around in circles not really talking at all. I felt like a lost little sheep day-dreaming the day away, hoping that any minute now Neil was going to pop his head round the corner and say "surprise......!" *It never happened, well he didn't.*

The hardest part of the whole day was knowing, when everyone had gone home, I would be home alone. I know my folks stayed for a few days, but when they finally left I was on my own. Every night I cried myself to sleep, it was hard to look at everything in the house, all of it just screamed Neil, from crazy duvet covers to the shelving units we picked out together, but he wasn't there. Learning how to live on your own is ok when the sun is up, but when the sun went down my heart followed every day.

Building a life after tragedy is not easy but I knew I would be ok, somehow.

Time has flown by. I cannot believe how fast it is going, it's a little scary really. I don't want to forget all the good stuff we did and all the fun times we had. I feel I need to remember: I often get my photo albums out just to jog my memory, they always make me laugh and make me cry without fail. From time to time when I'm super stressed or in a lot of pain, I dream about Neil and he lifts my spirits, he lets me know he's ok and happy, and he always encourages me to keep living. I know that may sound a little crazy, but we all have our ways of finding peace and over the years, I have slowly found mine.

As I am finishing this chapter, it just happens to be the 5th anniversary of Neil's passing, 28th October, and in my mind I am trying hard to remember the good times. There were so many good times, but those sad moments of the day we lost him still continue to creep in.

I know when you read this you'll be thinking .......yeah it sounded hard but you managed... well I can tell you now that I didn't really, I am still in shock and from time to time I get lost in my memories. I do not know if you have ever seen someone take their last breath of air. Well I have, and that is not something you forget in a hurry.

Sweet loves Mr. Smith, if you're watching me xxx

# 12 ON REFLECTION

Looking over my time with Neil, I wouldn't change a thing, even to this day I miss him dearly. It was quite evident that our relationship wasn't easy, I'm not really sure we really spent a great deal of time on our own, as there was always something or someone with us.

I have many memories about my time with Neil, some I would like to forget – the pain and suffering, some I love to remember – our wonderful wedding and sadly some that are fading – our holidays and days out.  My photos sometimes help but there were times I just wanted to hear his voice.  I know Neil is happy for me now but I will never forget about him.

My most difficult memories from my time with Neil are from the evenings. Neil was very stubborn and when it came time to go to bed, he would do whatever he could in his power not to go. It was my job to single handedly get him upstairs and ready for bed, which generally took me an hour or so. From pills to changing, he resisted me, I knew why but I couldn't change it or take away the pain.

At times I would get a shake on my shoulder at 2am in the morning to say, "I'm not feeling so good, can you take me to hospital?!" Obviously I jumped into action and took him straight away, but when you've gotta be at work at 9am the next morning it became difficult. I don't like to use the word resent, but I resented the cancer for hurting Neil and ruining my life. Watching my husband go through treatment hurt so much, I cannot imagine what my folks went through watch me during treatment; some people said it is harder to lose a child than a partner. I could argue with that, I think grief is hard no matter what or who you lose. When you love someone and they are taken away from you without a choice, it's hard.

On reflection I wish my folks had lived closer at the time, as when I went home I didn't have any support. Where Neil's folks had each other and his friends could stick together, I went home alone. At night, I cried a lot and I know that sounds soppy, but I didn't really have anyone to talk to and I needed to talk from time to time. There were quite a few people who said "Caz, you can come round anytime..." "Call me if you need anything!" Well when you're in that position you don't call because you don't want to be a bother, and sometime it's hard to pluck up the courage to take those steps.

When I see photos of Neil taken during his treatment, you can see him progressively getting worse during each round of chemo, I would have done anything to swap places with him and take away his pain. Going through Neil's treatment with him has had a lasting impact on me, I fear that I will lose my life again and I am not sure I could pick up the pieces for the third time. I know I wasn't there at the beginning of his treatment, when he first got diagnosed, and he had radiotherapy, but I know how treatment makes you feel, I understand pain and I know that feeling of guilt when it's all over, and you know you've just put your family through hell…. hearing his stories made me cringe.

Going through all of this with Neil has scarred me on top of the scars I had previously collected. It was rough, it was tiring, it was most definitely scary, my heart broke every day while I crumbled into a million pieces…. but I still wouldn't change it; he was my husband and he will always have that title. Every anniversary and birthday I will continue to take flowers to him, as I know he loves his carnations, and whilst I have my dinner with him, I will tell him everything that's going on with me and make sure he is ok. Yes…. I am fully aware I sound like a crazy person, but life is too short to worry what others think. I take peace in knowing he is ok and not hurting anymore. I am just sad in the knowledge that he will never experience any more of the world and the life he could have had. I will look after his mum and dad, Anne and Harry, forever. They will always be a part of my life, and I need them as much as they need me….. "For better, for worse, in sickness and in health!"

I will be there….. Love you guys.

# 13 SECOND CHANCE LIFE

Now I know you're thinking, "You've had a hard life" "It must have been difficult" and even "Do you think about it much?" Well......

It's no one's fault that I got cancer and I truly believe that it was just a random act of Mother Nature, no one could have predicted it was going to happen. I believe that this was how my life was meant to be and if I couldn't accept this then I know that life would be even harder than it already is. At 17, I learnt the true answer to the ultimate question..... "What is life? And how precious is it really?"

There are many things we take for granted in life and I have learnt the importance of how the little things we quarrel over really do not matter anymore. Don't get me wrong, I have my days where I get up and I'll have a little tantrum about something silly, like how they get the Teflon coating to stick to a non-stick pan. But I really do understand the meaning of life now and I'm pretty sure there are not many people at my age that can actually say that.

My family are a really big part of life and I know without them I would not be here today. During the last 10 years, they have picked me up when I have been down and kept me going strong when times were moving really fast. The strength and courage they have given me has made coping with cancer so much easier. I know it has been hard for them and I give thanks every day for them being in my life.

My mum and dad (John and Joan Coleman) are the kind of people who, when I was in hospital would not just look after me but they helped my friends when their folks couldn't get in during the day. They really are special people, even just thinking about them gives me a lump in my throat. And the number of times my brother Brian has looked after me is unbelievable. If you could have seen us as little kids you would not think that we would have such a close relationship today.

However, the look on his face was priceless when he walked in to see my bald head over a bucket with blood pouring from my nose like a tape... oh how glad we are those days are behind us now. Brian was great at taking me out on days I was feeling ok, he would help wrap me up in blankets, stick me in my wheel chair and would push me to town so I could get some fresh air. He treated me like normal and didn't walk on eggs shells like everyone else. He really is the best brother money could buy!

I have spent a lot of time thinking about how to thank the people in my life who have helped me get through my battle, and I am sure it will take me a life time to get through them all. Nevertheless, I decided that raising money for the TCT is the best way to thank everyone and help the teenagers and young people suffering today.
Unfortunately, some of those teens will not win the battle, and knowing this just makes me more determined to keep going.

Our first money-raising venture was selling a book of poems by Neil Smith. He put a book together before he passed away. He called it "Escaping the Demons" and during my grieving process, I felt the need to get his book printed in his memory.  We made approximately £5500, all of which we sent to the unit where Neil was treated in Sheffield, and they used the money to purchase new furniture and games for the patients.  We have since gone on to organise a sponsored walk, which sounded like a great idea at the time but was extremely hard for me. I had to use my crutches for most of the 17.7 miles.  My friends and family were happy to help and as a team we raised £4597. The day was amazing: we walked from Chesterfield town centre to The Weston Park Hospital in Sheffield. The atmosphere was electric and everyone was so supportive, we had a couple of local businesses involved and the sun shone all day.

Although The Teenage Cancer Trust has helped my medical situation, I feel as though my family were the ones who saved my life. They believed in me and that was all I needed to get through it all.

My dad even arranged for me and my friend Claire a go on Ready Steady Cook after our treatment. He believed in us that much, he knew we were going to get through everything and that kept us going. All we ever talked about whilst on chemo was what food we were going to eat and keep down when we got out.... It was like we were preparing to leave prison at times!

I have lost a lot through this disease. I believe my life will never be the same again. There are times where I do not feel as though I will ever have normality, however there are times where I do not want normality. I never thought that I would have experienced so much in these last 10 years and as clichéd as it sounds, I have found it difficult to put into words the emotions I have been through. My doctors say I'm cured now, though the label cancer will never leave me. I will always be that girl who had cancer or Caroline the one with the metal leg. How do I feel about this? I'm not sure.

Cancer has given me an opportunity to be my true self, although I do wonder from time to time who I would be without it. Would I still be that shy girl who just did what she was told, or would I put my foot down???? I'll never know!

Now when I was first diagnosed, people gave me coping strategies on how to deal with cancer, from leaflets to personal advice, but one thing I have learnt along the way is that there is no right or wrong way of dealing with cancer, it's just your way. There is no rulebook when it comes with dealing with cancer, no amounts of information will help anyone. I took each day as it came, and I am fully aware that my super powers enabled me to fight like a trooper but some people do struggle.

During my time on the ward, I tried my hardest to help as many of my friends as possible when they needed it, either to be uplifted or just relaxed to watch a movie. Helping other people seemed to work for me, there were occasions I had to enlist a little help from the parents, there may been a need for chocolate at times but I always tried to keep everyone going.

I chose my path and, yes, I can tell you my experiences, however no two experiences are the same. No matter how big or small cancer is, it is still cancer and that label comes with a lot of mental suffering.

Many people have said, "you're so strong," "you're so brave," "you're so this, that and the other," "how do you cope?" How I manage to get up every day and soldier on through the pain and mental stress that scares me to death, is to just...... get up and get on with it.

There are people in the world who will never get the chances and experiences that I have had and I have no right to moan.....! I have always said if you can get up and do something to change a problem, just do it, don't moan about it and if you can't change it.... just get on with life, it's precious! Life is for the taking, but we do the choosing.

Some days are difficult, not just because of my own cancer or Neil's, but every day I have a constant reminder in my leg. Over the last 10 years, the pain has increased and one day I know what will happen to my leg, but for now I will just keep having little MOT surgeries to keep my going. I would just like to keep my leg for as long as possible before they chop it off.... Briggsy, PLEASE!

Believe me, I am not super human, we all have bad days. I have days where I feel lost, as though the world expected me to die and that's why there's no life plan set out for me..... Woe is me!!! These days are my bad days and I know it is because I find it hard to deal with the fact that life after cancer is not what I expected.

I have survived cancer and I am totally lost some days, but I now have a wonderful husband called Angel who I love dearly and every day he keeps my head above water and without him, I think I would be in a crazy house. I have a fear that it's going to happen all over again and I am going to lose him, but I truly know he will always there for me.

Just so you all know, no one will ever replace my Mr. Smith, he was one in a million. Our past is what defines us, we should not forget it but live with it. I never thought I'd ever meet anyone new, I always felt that no one would be able to understand the relationship I have with Neil, and he will always be a big part of my life. But then things changed.....

Angel and I met in 2007; we both entered a competition to be in a charity calendar for a breast cancer helpline, which was put on by our local radio station and the listeners voted as to whom they wanted in it.

Angel lost his mum to breast cancer in the July of the same year I had lost Neil in the October of 2006. Individually we both felt strongly about the cause so when we entered the competition we wanted to win.

There were 10 girls and 10 boys chosen and not only did both Angel and I get a spot, we won in our categories, though I beat him over all by a good 200 votes. We didn't actually meet until they launched the calendar in the beginning of November, right at the end of the night. I was with my girlies and it was time to go home, and as I reached to put my empty bottle on the table, I stood on a foot, and turned to apologise, now we're married.....

The night we met was a little messy. I have to admit that I am not a big drinker, it doesn't take a lot for me to get tipsy, but that night I really went for it. I suppose it was like my last hurrah for Neil, to finally finish my goodbyes. When I had bumped into Angel, it didn't feel like an accident, for me it felt like Neil had pushed me in the right direction, towards a little bit of happiness.

Angel and I talked for hours that night, my friends eventually went home and then his friends followed shortly after. It felt so natural, kind of like we had known each other for years. When it was finally time to go home, Angel being the gentleman he is, he offered to take me home in a taxi, which I thought was nice. Unfortunately when we finally got to my front door I couldn't find my keys..... Oh dear..... not only could I not find my keys I had completely lost my handbag!!

My neighbour commented to me a few days later that I was a little dramatic whilst shouting.... "I can't get in my house..." repeatedly, in between projectile vomiting across my front lawn on my one and only good knee.... What must Angel have thought... I know I was mortified.... He is such a gent, he let me borrow his sofa that night, and when I finally got my spare key off Anne and Harry the next day, I had to rush to get ready for work, stupidly I left Angel on my sofa sleeping. It was weird I really felt safe, I knew he wasn't going to steal my tele or anything.

My mum is probably going to tell me off for leaving a complete stranger in my house with a set of keys!... However that day become even more embarrassing when Angel turned up at my work. All the girls were trying to get a sneaky peak while we were talking; he was bringing my keys back, which was a massive relief.

Any other ordinary chap would have just dropped off the keys and ran, but he explained he had been to town looking for my handbag but had no luck. So he went to the phone shop and got me a little phone handset, and when he passed it to me and said... "if you don't have a phone, I can't call you!" He had also put ten pounds credit on it. It was super romantic, all the girls at work let out a little... "ahhhhhh, that's so sweet". As he left, my heart was all fluttery, I felt so confused. I was having feelings that I had not felt for some time and it was kind of scary.

As the day came to an end, my friend Cheryl and I were sat eating pizza whilst getting ready to go out for the night. To be honest, neither of us really wanted to go as we were both still feeling it from the night before, but it was a birthday do so we thought we'd show face..... As we sat noshing on our meat feast, a phone started ringing, as I had lost mine I kinda just thought it was Cheryl's phone and she couldn't be bother to answer it.... I said "you not getting that...?" She replied, "my phone's off!" my heart went crazy.... It was him....

Angel was ringing on that phone he had bought me.....
What?????!!! Cheryl said, "quick answer it!" so I ran to the
hand set and said "Hello!" My mind went blank and I just
didn't know what to say, but thankfully Angel did all the
talking. He started with "Hello Miss May, now I'm not really
sure on dating protocol or how long I am supposed to leave
it before I ring you... I just thought fuck it, so here we are, on
the phone, talking.... Now are you busy tomorrow night? I
would like to take you out for dinner!" OMG, I've not been
on a date for years.... I just said.. "err... yes," "good" he said
"I'll pick you up at 7, I know where you live so be ready." For
the rest of the night that was all I could think about. Cheryl
had to put up with me all night, worry about what to wear
and foods I should steer clear from.....like things with too
much garlic, lol.

Wow, I was going on a date, it felt strange as I had to get
myself dressed up for someone new. I had to make myself
look sexy, now I am the biggest goofball and sexy does not
really suit me! After much deliberation and several outfit
changes, I went for something comfy, with a little bit of
sauce, it was a date after all. When he picked me up, my
stomach was in knots, I knew I was going to have a great
time but I felt so much guilt..... in my head all could think
was 'am I really doing this or is this all just a dream'.... Angel
hadn't booked a restaurant, which I thought was quite risky,
but we just drove round until we found somewhere to eat.

After a while I started to relax and really enjoy myself. As we
had both taken part in the calendar, we knew a little bit
about each other, I didn't have to explain myself to him,
and that felt nice. He knew about my leg, he knew about
Neil and he was cool with all of it.

151

From that date, I was hooked. We had a date every night that week and pretty much every other night after that. One day he turned up for dinner and never went home, we had fallen for each other and our lives became one. Our courtship was short but for some reason we both knew it was right....

.... I will say one thing about Angel; he respects my life I have had with Neil, and with that he understands that Anne and Harry are important to me, he even asked them for my hand in marriage.... Super sweet!

# 14 TEN YEARS ON AND I'M STILL LEARNING

To this day, I still go to clinic. I have to go once a year to have a check up on my metal work and once a year to make sure my lungs are happy. When the time comes to go, I get a little nervous but I know Briggsy and Jezza know exactly what they are doing.

However, there are a few questions have always bugged me, and during these visits I always hope to get answers........ Were they expecting me to live/get this far?? How long will this metal work really last?? Was it put in as a temporary measure so that I have two legs until the end?.... Never have I had answers..... Hmmmm…

I have slowly realised that life after teenage cancer is pretty lame. No one really knows what to say to you when you ask questions…. For example, I have many medical problems which have been diagnosed since I have finished my treatment. Take my asthma; over the years it has got worse and now I have to take steroid inhalers..... Has it got worse due to the tumours in my lungs or the chemo??? There doesn't seem to be a definitive answer, just a shrug of the shoulders. I know there are not many patients that get this far and I am super happy but these questions will always get to me.

As for my metal work, I call him Bertie. I believe it's a him as he causes me a lot of pain and discomfort. As we do not really know how long he is going to last, it has been vital I have a few MOT procedures to keep him functioning properly.

During 2008, I had to have a re-bushing procedure, where they replaced a couple of polyethylene bits (plastic bits!), which stabilise my knee to stop it from bowing in and causing more discomfort. When they told me I had to have this procedure done, I was kind of crapping myself.... They were planning on cutting me open again, all my memories flooded back....

OMG that was so painful last time. I was super scared, my heart sank, my nerves ran wild and to be honest I was a little angry...... However, I was in a lot of pain already so what could be worse, and this time I am an adult, so I had to be grown up and just suck it in.... Arrrggghhh.... The procedure went well, but the pain didn't really go completely. It made me wonder....

How many other procedure am I going to have to go through??? And am I over using Bertie?? They say that I have to be careful…. All I say to that is "I've stared death in the face, I'm super woman and you want me to be careful….. I don't think so!" I have the ethos of 'try it once and if you can do it… go for it… and if you can't then have a rest'!  At present I am on count down for procedure number 2. I am having a new kneecap; for some reason metal rubbing on bone is not a good thing…. It REALLY hurts!! I have 7 days to go, I am super nervous but I've got my brave face on and I've made a plan of action….. Suit case is packed and my list of stuff to pick is ready!!  I'm not sure how my family are feeling, they kind of just say the same things, like make sure you pack enough pants and socks…… etc.

No one ever says how they really feel, so I suppose that's why I am the way I am.  They probably feel like they would be stressing me out more than I need to be, but sometimes it would be nice to know I'm not the only one shitting myself…. Another cut in my leg, another set of staples to add to the collection and a new set of crutches……. I'm pretty sure that Briggsy never mentioned any of this stuff when he put Bertie in my left leg. I'm sure he never mentioned the amount of pain I would have as time goes on…… More unanswered questions!!!

There are many other long-term side effects, which they do not really talk to you about…. I am going to tell you about my fertility situation, as I believe that this a real important subject when it comes to teenage cancer and it's another area where there are very few answers.  Half way through my first cycle of chemotherapy the nurses asked me about my periods. I was a little embarrassed but nevertheless I explained that they had stopped. I was then asked how I felt about my fertility chat..... Hmmm... I replied with "I have no idea what you are talking about..." She then said "OH" I knew that face wasn't good. I then found out that they were supposed to talk to me about my eggs and what the chemo was going to do to them before they pressed the start button!.... Which they failed to do! Very unimpressed!!!

To this day I still do not know if my eggs would work or if my body even wants me to have a baby. Now I would be the first person to say that "I am not really maternal," but is that because of the chemo, is it fear of putting a child through what I have been through, or was I never destined to have little sprogs...? Another unanswered question!! It would seem that the further away from cancer you are the harder it becomes.... Maybe someone reading my story will understand that aftercare is important and needs to be re-addressed.

I would love to help as many teenagers and young adults as possible to survive their cancer. During my last clinic appointments for both oncology and surgery, I was asked if I would donate my notes for medical research. I jumped at this chance to help; I gave my X-rays, my scans, my blood, my tumor and all my notes. I hope one day they find a cure for cancer. I'm not so naive to think that is going to happen in the next ten years, but maybe in generations to come they will be able to rid the world of this awful disease.

I want to give my story a happy ending, but there is no real ending, I am still trying to live my life, surviving is hard and there are not many of us out there! And that may all sound a little dramatic, but I'm doing ok and that's pretty much it. I am beginning a new chapter of my life with my wonderful husband Angel and super sweet step daughter Maddie, and as hard as I try for cancer to not be a part of it, I know that most days I will have a thought for my cancer and of the people I have loved and lost.

The percentage of teenagers who survive cancer and who make it to where I am is not many, and when I start a new day I start it with meaning. Life is moving on and Angel and I will continue to celebrate Neil and My wedding anniversary on the 21st Jan, and the day he died, 28th Oct, as a mark of respect and to remember the happy times. Honestly, I do not want to forget my life. I am only human and we are not all perfect, I know that most people reading this will relate to some parts of my life and that's ok.......

Life for me now is totally different. I have just recently completed my level 5 Certificate of Education, which enables me to teach at college level. I am sure Mr. O'Reilly would be proud. I now have a job working in our local college, helping students with dyslexia like myself and also working with students who have behaviour issues. I find this really rewarding and with a new-found passion for education, I am reading more books and so far, I'm writing my own lol! I feel as though I have much more to learn and will continue as long I can.

Hmmmmm.....

It's funny, I have got to the end of my story and I have just realised that I am normal, which I never thought was possible. I have those same day to day struggles as everyone else, and maybe telling my story was what I needed to keep me going for another 10 years.

Thanks for reading x

# 15 MY THANK YOU'S, TO ALL THAT HAVE INSPIRED ME

Here are just a few people I want to thank for all the wonderful things they have done for me over the years!

To all the guys at the TCT, I owe you my life, not just for providing us all with these wonderful units but for everything else you have given me. Oh and I don't just mean you guys who get paid lol... but I mean all the wonderful people I have met through the TCT. I have my purpose in life now and I don't think I'd ever be where I am if it wasn't for all I have learnt from you lot.

Mr. Roger Daltrey, who has done so much to the TCT over the years. When I first met him, he gave me the experience of a life time and I can't thank him enough. This was my first 'The Who' concert with all my friends.

This special man is Angelicas with Susie and Big T. I spent my
first Find your Sense of Tumour with him, he inspired me to be
myself and free spirited, and he holds a special place in my
heart as he always had fun and a huge smile on his face.
Rest in peace my friend.

The wonderful Ryan and Bianca, who have helped me so much over the years, from them I have learnt some many different things about life. Sadly, Ryan lost his battle to cancer but his memory will always live on in all of us. 'B' helped me through my own loss and for that I will be in debt forever... babes you will always be a part of our family.

Well Susie, I never thought in a million years that we would ever get here, but we did. You are the most amazing person I have ever met and in our eyes, as a family, you will always be a part of our lives. We love you and we thank you from the bottom of our hearts.... And yes I know I've got soppy in my old age!!!

Mr. Nigel Revel sees the best in people, he is such a lovely man and kept Neil and I going over the years! "Thank you" for helping all of us realise we can make it through all this crap and come out the other side stronger than ever.

Des Murphy is an amazing man with a not just a heart of gold, but a pure soul which radiates like the sun. He had done so much for Neil during the last years of his life that my family and I regard him quite highly for that. Even to this day, Anne sometimes wells up when we talk about the times that Neil spent with Des. "Des, Thank you, you will never really understand how much we appreciate all you do for us and the TCT"

To Laura and Super Bev (Beverly), we have spent many TCT concerts together helping out and doing our bit. You both inspire me to achieve and my thanks comes from myself and Neil, as I know he watches over all of us. You are both wonderful people and hold a place in my heart....Big Hugs.

And all you lot!!!!

My Family are wonderful; I have a mum and dad who have always been there for me and always will be. My brother is amazing, he has so much in his life but still has time for me. I love them all dearly.

My family extends quite a long way, my besy friend Lisa is like a sister to me, she listens to me babble on regular basis on the phone and she has been there for me over the last 10 years.  Big hugs my lovely xx

And to extend my family even further, Neil's parents are still a big part of my life, they live round the corner from me and I will always see them as my in-laws. I know this is what Neil would have wanted.  They do so much for me and I can't thank them enough.

And to my new family, Angel my now and wonderful husband who has taken on all of me and my baggage, and let me tell you now my baggage is very heavy... and Maddie my very cute step daughter, although she is growing up quicker than I can keep up with......

That's me, I hope I have inspired you to live with strength and ambition.

## THE END

# MY DEDICATION TO MR NEIL SMITH

As I mentioned, Neil wrote many poems and I would like to share with you a few of my favorites and a couple of Anne and Harry's too. Neil always wanted to get his work out there to "Inspire the World" and this is my dedication to him.

## She

For she is beauty, for she is life
Ever faithful and ever loyal
She will make this lucky guy
The most beautiful and perfect wife

A ray of light on a cloudy day
The sparkle in the rain
Her form is class and beauty within
She deserves a life without pain

A soul mate I can call my own
For this I have never had
She walks in beauty, she walks in light
She keeps me warm, on the coldest night

Her bright blue eyes, her perfect smile
The kindness that comes naturally
Always giving, always caring
For she is beauty, for she is life

©Neil Smith 2004

## Any Time...

Any time you feel the pain
Just walk outside into the rain
Beg the sun to shine on through
That's really all you have to do.

Any time you feel the stress
Can't get up – your hair's a mess
Take a shower, put on a smile
That'll keep you going for a while.

Any time you're feeling low
The worlds against you – its weight in tow
Don't give up – it's up to you
Is that really all you need to do?

## Wake me when it's over

The sleepless nights that never pass
The painful days have no sympathy
A crowded room of white and black
Wake me when it's over

A bang on the wall, a scream, a shout
Waiting for the light to go out
Another day down, how many to go?
Wake me when it's over

The hurt that makes my days so slow
Yet there is comfort in this pain
Tomorrow will come, same eyes, new hope
Wake me when it's over

The needle that punctures my skin with angst
To fill my veins with poison
It travels around – a killing machine
Wake me when it's over

The corridor light – the watchful eyes
They come to check on me
I'm not asleep, it's not a dream
Wake me because it's over

©Neil Smith 2003

## Endless

One day at a time

My salvation, I cannot find

To see what's left behind

My lord, give me a sign.


I watch the moon at night

I stare into its eyes

To awaken the fire inside

My lord, give me a sign.


Again I'm in a bind

One wish – a peaceful night

To sleep away the pain

My lord, give me a sign.

## **Peace at Last**

Silent eyes and sympathy

Nothing calm ever waits for me

To carry the cross that judges me

Feelings now that won't let me be


The time of day that awakens me

Points of view that I cannot see

I hear the voices that worry me

Why oh why, won't they let me be


The silent stone that comforts me

That keeps me safe and cares for me

Eyes are fixed but they cannot see

Maybe now at least they will let me be

# WHY DID I WRITE MY BOOK???

When I made it to the beginning of my 10th year I had a tattoo, on my neck, to celebrate my life and what I have achieved,

I spent a lot of time reminiscing about all my experiences and what I had been through. I started making notes, just so I don't forget the exciting life I have had and eventually those notes have now turned in a book about me.

I want to inspire people who believe they cannot achieve anything in life. I want them to believe that there is hope out there and no matter what you go through in life, with a bit of strength and courage anything is possible. This book is not just for cancer patients or their families, it is for anyone who has lost their faith in life and needs some inspiration.

I want to make my reader smile, cry, think, and feel invincible....

When I had made it to the end of the 10th year off treatment, I felt elated as I had achieved something that I and my doctors could not have imagined. I needed closure and to celebrate this milestone, so I decided that as I couldn't see the tattoo on the back of my neck, I would have one I could see to remind me to keep on going...

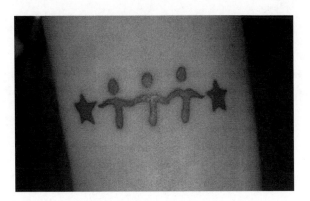

My book is not meant to be a long read, it is a short story about a stage in my life where I have overcome major trauma and come out the other side on top!

Thank you

# FINAL THANK YOU'S

Some very big thank you's I would like to put out there,

Firstly to my wonderful husband for encouraging me to do this in the first place, writing this book has really helped my mental state and also help him understand what my life has been like.

To  Rachel Sabian-Farrell for helping me with my grammar and punctuation, ensuring that my excessive use of comers and full stop's didn't make your head spin as your were reading,

And finally to Harriett Buckely for taking a very cool photo for my front cover, I hope you are pleased with the result too.

4048620R00106

Printed in Great Britain
by Amazon.co.uk, Ltd.,
Marston Gate.